Saturdays With Bob
Life Changing Golf Lessons for Mind, Body and Spirit

Gena Living

Saturdays With Bob:

Life Changing Golf Lessons for Mind, Body and Spirit

Copyright © 2015 Gena Livings

All rights reserved. No portion of this book may be reproduced mechanically, electronically, or by any other means, including photocopying, without written permission of the author. It is illegal to copy this book, post it to a website, or distribute it by any other means without permission from the author.

"Saturdays With Bob," "Life Changing Golf Lessons" and Angel Bob logo are TradeMarks of Gena Livings.

ISBN: 978-0-9826193-1-5

Gena Livings
Gena@ GenaLivings.com
http://www. GenaLivings.com

Author photo by Marie Clark

All other photos courtesy of author

Dedication

I dedicate this book to you, Dear One, with the loving intention that, by applying these life changing golf lessons, you will experience all of the joy, peace and happiness from 'within' when you step into your power and put the Highest Good to work in your daily life.

This is a true story and I am sharing my experiences with you as I remember them. Some of the events in this narrative, however, have been compressed to facilitate the telling of my story.

I have written personal letters to you at the end of each lesson hoping to provide you with further insights, thoughts and reflections from my current vantage point.

The lessons you are about to receive were a gift given to me in 1992 and I have come to appreciate that life is all about individual perception. What one person interprets may be completely different from what another person in the same situation may interpret and/or experience. It all depends on how our individual thoughts, feelings, and behaviors shape our world.

May this profoundly impact you in some way as it did me so many years ago!

Table of Contents

Introduction 7

I am a Painting..11

Chapter 1: The War...15

Chapter 2: First Meeting 33

Chapter 3: Follow Your Intuition.................................39

Chapter 4: Finding Purpose..49

Chapter 5: Focus and Silence 65

Chapter 6: Choose Happiness 77

Chapter 7: Friendship – Surround Yourself with Positive People 93

Chapter 8: Positive Self-Talk 99

Chapter 9: Creating Confidence by Visualizing Your Outcomes 113

Chapter 10: Self Love and Acceptance........................... 125

Chapter 11: Be True, Be You...................................... 133

Chapter 12: Be Grateful 141

Chapter 13: Experience Nature 153

Chapter 14: Good Nutrition....................................... 165

Chapter 15: Healthy Exercise—the Final Lesson... 175

Chapter 16: Conclusion 183

Gratitudes... 189

Introduction

As I journey through this adventure called life, I often encounter people who are full of negativity toward their childhood experiences or their parents whom they blame for their present state in life.

I have found, through my own inner-work and healing, that blaming our past experiences and/or our parents for our struggles only keeps us *stuck* in angry, anxious, and depressed feelings and interferes with our ability to discern what we could do differently *today* to make our lives more positive, more productive, and more powerful.

I would like to humbly share some of my childhood experiences in the opening chapter of this book so that you, my honorable reader, can see how *Bob's Life Changing Golf Lessons* gave me the tools to shape my future and to move my life forward in the spirit of love and forgiveness in order to create a healthier, happier, and more positive outlook in my own life.

Because of my teacher's compassionate and loving insights, I've learned and embodied within myself that healing our relationship with our earthly creator(s) (our parents) also heals our relationship with our Heavenly Creator (God—The Living Spirit—that dwells within us all).

Today, I love life, and I am free to do what I love by expressing myself through writing, wellness coaching, and inspiring others to achieve a lifestyle that promotes health, happiness, creativity, and spiritual well-being.

I have realized—thanks to my parents and to my teacher and mentor Bob and his *Life Changing Golf Lessons*—that everything we experience is an opportunity to challenge us in our personal growth, reach our highest self, and strive for spiritual well-being.

It is my sincere belief that God is always rooting for our success and intends for us to reach our full potential so we can live complete and fulfilled lives. We must allow the Divine energy *within* us to help guide us in becoming more *conscious* of our daily choices that lend to more positive, productive, and powerful outcomes.

When you read about my childhood you will see that sometimes *life is just plain messy*, not always happy, bright, and beautiful, but if you look closer, you will also notice how life in its most messy state is what eventually brings out the beauty and the light *within* us all.

Over the years, I have learned that happiness is not always a place that we arrive *at*, but instead, a place that we *get to* once we make up our mind to just *BE* there.

If you find only one nugget of wisdom from the *Life Changing Golf Lessons* presented in this book, it will have been worth the effort sharing it with you.

There is a beautiful Indian expression used as a greeting or upon parting, by putting the palms of the hands together in prayer position. It means, *"I honor the Spirit in you which is of love, of truth, of light and of peace. When you are in that place in you and I am in that place in me, we are one."*

I am a Painting

*I am paint on the end of God's brush
that covers white canvas with the stroke of His touch.*

*I am unique in creation and design,
only the artist can alter my line.*

*I am different from that of the norm;
I want to fit in but I cannot conform.*

*I am not a Picasso or Rembrandt by name,
but I am an original by no less claim.*

*I am a question, therefore I ask,
What is my purpose? What is my task?*

*I am not boastful, proud or vain,
but modest and humble, I will remain.*

*I am a believer in all that is good;
I need not be understood.*

*I am imagination that continues to grow,
visions of color, in endless flow.*

*I am Truth on a white canvas board;
I hold up my promise on every accord.*

*I am an opinion in a soft spoken voice,
displaying my colors, stating my choice.*

*I am a crafter of tints and hues,
through perils and struggles; I'll stand by my views.
I am open to many, and some may oppose,
because I embrace strangers, sinners, and foes.*

*I am a friend that will never judge,
persecute any, or hold a grudge.*

*I am a promise to those who see;
take my hand and walk with me.*

*I am laughter behind a tear,
never showing hints of fear.*

*I am an expression of self and soul,
my colors are vivid, yet sometimes dull.*

*I am still in memory fade,
belief in truth, my soul is made.*

*I am roses, I am love,
peaceful mind, soaring dove.*

*I am the sky, velvety blue,
always giving, always true.*

I am the grass, emerald green,
animals, trees, honey-bees.

I am a mountain, ocean breeze,
preserving "nature's" salt bed seas.

I am a garden, strawberry wine,
sweet red grapes from a succulent vine.

I am a painting withered and old;
quest and purpose begin to unfold.
I am a story, my message is clear;
now the time is drawing near.

I am eternity in spirit and mind;
my memory and legacy, left behind.

I am "God's" paint for all to see;
my Love to give,
was my reason to be.

~Gena Livings~

CHAPTER 1
The War

Have you ever wondered why you are here? What is your purpose in life, the one you were born to fulfill?

Actually, this was one of my biggest questions I faced growing up, and I prayed to God every single day that he would provide me with the answer. I was a very spiritual child filled with an intense longing to know God and kept what I called my *Poem Journal*.

But my early childhood was a *war*. I tiptoed on a religious and domestic mine-field.

> *Dear God,*
> *My life is a battlefield when faced with confusion.*

I am the youngest of seven children and the only girl. Being raised in an army of men was like being drafted into the Vietnam War. I didn't really have a choice. I had to be tough in order to survive.

Our family lived in a war zone *The End Days* as my parents (primarily my dad) believed. The particular church to which we belonged taught its members to believe this and everyone bought into this belief! It's true that if we allow others to think for us and define who we are, we are giving them the power to dictate where our path will lead us.

Photo of Mom, my brothers, and me around our family dinner table.

The War was a battle of *religious differences* between my mom and my dad. My brothers and I were soldiers fighting for our lives and country. Mom and Dad were our country; they were our law and our God. We believed in them, and so we did what all good soldiers do -- we fought in *their* war. Their battles weren't bloody, but they launched verbal grenades at each other which sent my brothers and me ducking for cover in our emotional trenches, fearing the fallout.

Dear God,
When I'm alone at night, silence speaks to me.

I hear the sounds a deaf man feels deep within himself.
My inner soul begins to tighten and all strength has flourished.
My mind wonders and all thought, too far to redeem.
The darkness grows in texture and tenseness dwells.
The feeling subsides when daylight's voice takes command.

This endless battle waged for as long as I can remember day after day, month after month, year after year. As the years passed, my older brothers left the war to start new lives for themselves. I was happy for them. I was also sad to see them go. I think they all deserve a medal of courage, but I guess some soldiers will forever go unnoticed.

Dear God,
Guided by a passage too dark to find my way—
but as each day passes
I get closer to the light.
Where will this passage take me?
How long before I find its end?

This early experience caused me to question God, my faith, my beliefs, and my own purpose for being. Even before Mom's attempted suicide, I experienced confusion and resentment simply because I couldn't understand *why* my parents would willingly bring me into the world *knowing* that they were dealing with so much personal conflict and unrest between them. I couldn't wrap my head around that when I was a kid, but I told myself that everybody's life has purpose, and I was sure to find mine someday.

This is why Bob and his life changing golf lessons would make such an impact on me later in my life. Mom and Dad had always provided similar insights while I was growing up, but I had difficulty seeing through the muddy conflict that clouded these lessons beyond recognition. I truly appreciate how Bob provided a new spin and a deeper, more loving perspective so that I could appreciate my parents and my experience in a new light as you will also come to learn in the following chapters.

*My older brother Bobbie and me. He made a swing from an old piece of wood and rope. He transitioned in 2001; I still feel his sweet presence surrounding me **every** day. I will always remember that **JOYFUL** moment when he gifted me with my very first **swing**.*

Dear God,

Why does my mind wonder so?

Do I think too much for my own good or is this normal to search until I find the correct meaning?

Am I supposed to walk this road alone?

I'll keep walking...

Who else will I see along the way?

Does anyone hear my voice?

I'll keep walking...

I don't have a destination but I can sense the way.

When will I know for sure?

I'll keep walking....

Was I born without given the choice to be here?

That doesn't make sense.

I'll keep walking...

If I chose to be here before my birth, I must already know something.

Is that what I sense?

I'll keep walking....

Does anyone hear my voice?

If I chose this human life, am I walking toward God?

Is this what I sense?

I'll keep walking....

I have to experience this!

Have I forgotten something?

Why can't I remember?

Why is it so hard?

Like a baby taking steps back to her mother.

She reaches for me but my legs are new and fragile

and the journey seems far.

Does anyone hear my voice?

The War Begins...

In 1953, my parents lived in a small apartment complex in San Francisco, California, when they joined a church that created turmoil and conflict in the early days of their marriage. Mom was a housewife, and Dad attended school and worked. They had only been married for a few months. Mom was pregnant with my oldest brother.

One particular evening Mom fixed a special dinner for Dad. When Dad returned home from work, he asked, "What's for dinner?"

"Pork chops," she said, proud and enthused.

Dad marched over to the stove, removed the pork chops from the oven, and threw them into the garbage. He told her that they were never going to eat pork again because eating pork was "against church doctrine." My mom, confused, said, "What church? What doctrine?"

Dad explained that he joined a church and had been attending its meetings for several months. My mom had *NO IDEA* that this was going on. In hindsight, I'm certain that my dad meant well by joining the church because of his desire to provide a spiritual foundation for his new family, but he certainly went about it in the *wrong* way, not knowing any better at the time. He later admitted to me how bad he felt about his early decisions and the grief it caused all of us.

Unfortunately, Dad never consulted Mom or gave her an

opportunity to voice her opinion about joining the church. Mom felt that Dad didn't respect her opinion and certainly wasn't sensitive to her feelings. She grew resentful and angry toward Dad early on in their marriage and that resentment toward him just built up over the years.

Several years and seven kids later, Mom remained a stay-at-home housewife, and Dad, at this point, owned and operated his own business. In order to do this, he had to spend a great deal of time at work, but he always made time for us kids and for our yearly backpacking trips. These were some of my fondest memories growing up.

Dear God,
On a mountaintop I can be taller than anyone
for a short moment in my life.
I can take in a breath of fresh air and feel the freedom that surrounds me.
I hear the sounds of nature's call and I answer with quiet thoughts.

Dad & me and our family dog, Hondo, Sierra Nevada Mountain Range

Mom and Dad became heavily involved in the church by this time, and Dad reached *Deacon* status, which was a pretty important position in the church. This church had very strict rules that had to be followed. For example, the church forbade its members to receive any kind of medical treatment by physicians. This terrified Mom because there were several instances over the years when we needed medical treatment, and we were not allowed to receive any. We were not allowed to celebrate any holidays like Christmas, Halloween, Easter, etc. And we weren't allowed to celebrate birthdays because it was considered a *sin* to *honor one's self*. Mom always baked us a cake anyway, and we celebrated our birthdays in *secret*.

My birthday celebration

This church instructed women to be *submissive* to their husbands. Women were not allowed to voice their opinions, especially about the church or the church elders. Families were required to give a *big* portion of their gross income in tithes away to the church, even if families were dirt poor. This was not an option.

My family and all of the church members lived with *FEAR* that we were living in the *End Times!* The followers of this church, which basically in the end was a *cult*, believed their leader was a *special* apostle/prophet sent by God to protect and deliver them from the Apocalypse. He promised his congregation deliverance to a place of safety (in Petra, Jordan) where only God's chosen people would be spared as the world crumbled and the rivers of fire burned up all non-church members to death. He also proclaimed that he would not die until Jesus returned back to earth. Well, he died.

Every church member was instructed to keep stockpiles of dried food in their basements as the end of the world loomed. Earthquakes, droughts, floods, and other natural disasters were signs of God's displeasure; he would destroy the world and those who resided outside of this *chosen* church. My parents lived in this fear-based belief system for years! But my mom finally had *enough* and took a stand against the church and its dogma.

She no longer wanted to be part of this church/cult or its strict teachings, doctrines, and practices, but she went along with my dad because she felt she had no other *choice* in the matter.

She had a slew of kids, no job, and nowhere else to go. At that time in her life, she felt *stuck* without any options, so she endured the situation until she just couldn't take it any longer. That's when she rebelled against the church. Things grew worse from there between Mom and Dad when she got kicked out for showing up to church one day wearing make-up, a short skirt, and smoking a cigarette. Since my dad was a *Deacon* in the church this obviously added fuel to the fire.

Mom and me at church

Everyone, including long-time friends in the church, turned their backs on Mom and banned her from participating in any outside social events during church gatherings. These people were her only friends. You weren't allowed to have close friends outside the church because they weren't considered *chosen* by God.

Instead, Mom took me to the park on weekends while Dad continued to take my brothers to church. All I know is that once Mom was kicked out of the church she wasn't going to allow Dad to have control over me her only daughter. She didn't want *any* of her children involved in that church, but for some reason, she put her foot down when it came to me.

I loved our outings at the park. Mom explained to me that this was our new *church*. She would pack a lunch, and we would eat under the trees. I would play on the swings and ride the train that circled the park. I enjoyed our new church it became my favorite event.

It became a place of peace and refuge for me outside the war, a kind of cease-fire. I could sense Mom's calm and serene disposition from within my own being, and this soothed my soul. At the park, her demeanor was always relaxed, joyful and carefree. I could feel this presence quieting my thoughts and releasing tension from my body. There was no struggle or inner conflict at the park -- only the swings blowing in the wind, the smell of fresh cut grass, the birds flying overhead, and the feeling of fresh air kissing my face which made me feel that everything would be *OK*.

> *Dear God,*
> *I ride on the wings of time. A bird carries me on his back,*
> *letting me see the world from above. Looking down, I see*
> *a world that is no longer a part of me and I, therefore,*
> *have no desire to return. I can only feel the wind.*

Two years after Mom was kicked out, the church broke up due to scandal, but they still have several splinter groups active today. When the church disassembled, my dad fell apart mentally, emotionally and spiritually. Dad left home on several different occasions and started having extramarital affairs. As a result of Dad's infidelities, Mom attempted suicide. I was nine years old.

After Mom's attempted suicide, I became her *sounding board*. With no one to talk to or express her feelings to, she vented her frustrations to me. At that time, it was too overwhelming for me to process my own feelings because I was only concerned about her feelings; I checked out emotionally. All I know is that I felt pain because she felt pain, I felt sadness because she felt sadness, and I felt despair because she felt despair. Like my mom, I didn't feel that I had anyone to talk to about what was going on in our home or our lack of a stable family life.

I lived in a constant state of worry, anxiety and stress. I felt that it was my main responsibility to take care of her and fill her emotional void due to the fact that my father was emotionally unavailable to her.

Although I was worried for Mom's safety and emotional well-being, I also felt angry and resentful toward her for wanting to leave me *behind* after she attempted suicide. It was difficult and very painful for me to understand why she would bring me into a world full of turmoil and disruption only to leave me stranded. I couldn't process all this confusion in my mind, so I slipped into my own world of self-protection and poured all my emotions into my *Poem Journal* and art projects as a way to release and express my feelings to God. I quietly withdrew into the world of creativity where I felt free and safe from the physical world that I was born into. I prayed to God through my poems as a way to release my feelings or to ask him a question. I wrote many poems to God in hopes that he would one day hear my voice and answer my longings.

Dear God,
Looking high into the sky,
I wait for your face to appear before me.
As I lay down to bed at night to pray,
I listen for your voice to speak back to me.
When I'm feeling empty and depressed,
I wait for your embrace to comfort me.
I am confused when you do not reveal yourself to me.
I often wonder about your existence and my purpose for being.

At that time, I grew angry and resentful toward my dad for driving Mom to the point of suicide and total desperation. When Mom was in the hospital, Dad took me out to dinner with his girlfriend. She followed me into the bathroom and tried to engage in an intimate conversation with me. I told her at that point, in no uncertain terms, to stay *AWAY* from my family, and that I wanted *NOTHING* to do with her! I think she was hoping that we would become best friends that night, but that just wasn't going to happen.

Dad and his girlfriend broke up very soon after that and Dad returned home to Mom and their war.

The War Erupts on a New Front…

A couple years after the church disassembled, Dad became a spiritual *explorer,* while Mom deepened her belief in the Christian Faith.

Dad's pursuit of *spiritual enlightenment* brought forth yet another *WAR* and a fresh new bag of ammunition.

Dad became interested in things like extraterrestrial activity and became a UFO investigator conducting interviews on UFO reports and sightings. He also became interested in the teachings of The Ascended Masters and all types of natural healing modalities like magnet therapy, Reiki, acupuncture, Chinese medicine and natural herbs. He also became fascinated with the realm of quantum physics.

I always felt stuck in the *middle* of my parents' fighting and I didn't know which side to pick, so I waved the *white flag* in order to keep peace and balance.

I realized that this was my parents' war and not mine to fight, so remaining *neutral* was my best defense.

When I was in high school, Mom and Dad still battled over their religious differences, but Dad was now diagnosed with early stages of onset Parkinson's disease.

At that time, Dad felt it important to prepare for his future health and well-being. He made arrangements to live at the Napa Valley Veterans Home where they could properly care for his disease, as it was certain to worsen over time.

Dad moved out of the house and into the Veterans Care Facility a few years after I graduated from high school. My dad struggled for many years with Parkinson's disease, but he found a place of peace within his Heart after much soul searching, forgiveness, surrender, and acceptance. Dad passed away in 2008 from complications with his Parkinson's disease. Dad was an amazing man and a true adventurer in both the spiritual realm and the physical realm. He always loved climbing a mountaintop in order to get a fresh new perspective. He always aimed *HIGH* and caught the next available ride out on a Shooting Star!

Mom remained at home and continued to work on her own emotional and spiritual healing. After much self-development work, Mom gained a strong sense of *self* and became fully *grounded* in her Christian faith. This faith empowered her physically, spiritually, and mentally. She returned to work and regained her independence and self-confidence. Mom became victorious in so many ways! She was a warrior of faith and released her shackles of fear. She overcame self-defeat and stood strong in her beliefs and principles. She was able to live freely in her new found strengths for a good many years. Then with very little warning, pancreatic cancer drafted Mom into a new battle. She succumbed to it in 2005.

I don't blame my parents for the decisions or choices they made in their life. They both made the best decisions they could with what they knew at the time. It's this process of learning and growing from our mistakes that makes up the fabric of our life. The situations in which they found themselves could happen to *anyone*.

I deeply desire that the pages in this book empower you to learn from your past experiences, not turn them into excuses or let them dis-empower you. I urge you not to become victimized by your past or to spend any energy blaming your parents for your childhood. These happenings are all part of daily life, learning, and growing. Begin living today in the present moment with the intention of moving forward in a new and powerful way!

Try to look at all your life experiences as an adventurous journey into the unknown bliss. When you look at life in this way, you don't expect perfect outcomes -- instead you allow all your imperfect outcomes to *BE* your perfection.

Somewhere between the darkness and the light, our mistakes and human foibles are all part of God's calling card to *WAKE US UP* and move us deeper into the *Energy of Love*.

My Earthly parents have both returned home into the womb of our Heavenly Creator where they are now joined together in the Light of The Eternal Flame.

Mom and Dad are forever loved in the Heart and Soul of their children and will be remembered in all future generations to come.

All of these events in my early childhood, which may seem unfair, difficult, sad, and sometimes insurmountable, have woven together the fabric of my being. These circumstances were the fertile ground that helped me to blossom, ripen, and grow. Out of the mud grows the lotus. But these events planted a firm conviction within me to reach out and help others who may have experienced, or may be experiencing, some of the same challenges.

New Beginnings

Looking back, my *second chance and new beginning* occurred when I was finally old enough to leave the war, and I went out and encountered a whole new world. I left home when I was 19 years old to begin my corporate career. I was figuring out my way in the world and landed a great job in Corporate America, mostly because I was *determined* to gain my independence early on in life. I still tried to make sense of my childhood and why things went down the way they did, and I wondered how to live my life in a way that would serve a higher purpose.

What I discovered when I left home was a world that was open, bright and beautiful. The possibilities were endless. It was a new emotional and spiritual beginning. God had painted a new picture for me on a fresh white canvas, and I could now *choose* the colors and experience life through a fresh lens.

Dear God,
My eyes are the window to my soul.
They see my destiny and guide me toward it.
My eyes see all the goodness of life and my soul is therefore content.

I was thankful for this new opportunity, and I wanted to explore this canvas and my place in it as much as possible. My quest led me to embrace life in a whole new way, thanks to an unassuming golf teacher with an unorthodox swing and his life changing golf lessons. He gave me some of the most incredible spiritual, yet practical guidelines for living an inspired life. I learned how to live my life in a way that would create wholeness, peace, and health from the inside out. The pages in this book are an attempt to capture the wisdom of my teacher, my mentor and my friend to whom I will be forever grateful.

Dear God,
A soul that travels the winds of time shall find the world of glory.
Let the mind dream and search for this paradise.
It shall be carried with the wind and You will be its guide.

First Meeting

In the spring of 1992, my dad called, asking if I would drive to Napa, where he lived. He wanted me to meet an unconventional golf teacher who had an uncanny swing. With childlike exuberance in his voice, he explained that the teacher's swing was *revolutionary* and unlike anything he'd ever witnessed before. He assured me that I would be captivated by this unique style and that I just had to experience it for myself.

Dad and I have always shared a common interest and appreciation for the game of golf.

I was in elementary school when Dad picked up some used golf clubs at a local garage sale for me to try out. I was thrilled! Dad taught me how to hit golf balls at the age of nine, and from that day forward golf became my sport of choice. Hitting golf balls in our backfield was a form of release for me; I could hit golf balls into the air and release all my worries and cares into the wind.

When I arrived at the golf range, the weather was unusually warm with strong head winds moving in from the North East bay of San Francisco. I noticed my father standing on the driving range talking to an older man with graying hair and a lean build.

When I approached them, the man standing next to my dad reached out for my hand and extended a warm welcome.

"Hello, you must be Gena. My name is Bob whether you say my name backwards or forward, I'm still 'good ole' Bob.'" We all laughed. I immediately warmed up to Bob's quirky sense of humor and friendly disposition. "Your father was just explaining to me that you drove all the way down here just to watch my golf swing!"

"I sure did. He told me that you have an unusual swing, unlike anything he's ever seen!"

"Well then I'll let you see for yourself," Bob said, grinning. His expression reminded me of a mischievous school boy. "I'm going to take a few practice swings, and I would like to know if you can figure out what I'm doing differently with my swing from what you typically see." At that point, Bob took a couple of steps back from where we stood and began taking a few practice swings with his club. He paused and asked, "So, what are you noticing so far?"

"I'm noticing that you are only using your upper body to complete the trajectory of your swing. You are not using your legs to drive through the ball. You are relying *solely* on your arms and hands to produce the power, and this is completely opposite of everything that I've ever been taught about how to swing a golf club," I explained.

"My, my…you are a quick study and absolutely right on target," Bob laughed. "I am, in-fact, relying solely on my upper body to produce the power through my shot, instead of using my legs. I believe that the golf swing is a lot like a suitcase into which we are trying to pack one too many things. I've learned over time that you just have to lighten the load in order to make things less complicated."

Bob took another practice swing, and I found myself watching him again. "Daily life is that way, too," he continued. "Now I'm going to hit a few balls so that you can get the full impact of the swing, once I make contact with the ball." At this point, my mind was absolutely spinning out of control at the very thought of this.

How can this be true? How can he possibly get any distance on the ball using only his upper body? I really didn't think he could possibly produce enough energy to power through his shot that way. It seemed completely impossible! As Bob approached the ball in preparation for his shot, I was certain he was not going to get any distance on the ball.

I watched him with spiked curiosity as he wound up his upper torso like a tight rubber band. On his downswing, he snapped through the ball and made perfect contact with the sweet spot. The ball soared through the headwinds, like a knife cutting through butter. He continued to hit ball after ball straight into the headwinds with perfect precision, unprecedented distance, and uncanny accuracy.

Completely awestruck, I was at a loss for words. I couldn't believe my eyes. "How did you learn to swing like that?" I asked in disbelief and excitement.

"Several years ago I was in a severe car accident that left me practically paralyzed from the waist down. I had to wear braces on both of my legs for three years during my rehabilitation period." He placed another ball on the tee and struck it through the air before continuing with his story.

"I made up my mind that I wasn't going to let the accident get the best of me or crush my spirit, so I focused on what *WAS* working for me instead of focusing on what wasn't working for me. My upper body *WAS* working for me, so I didn't let my legs stand in the way, pardon the pun, of my golf game." He finished demonstrating his incredible golf swing and leaned on his club. I moved in closer to focus on his explanation.

"I practiced for hours on end, trying to find ways to perfect my swing using only my upper body. By focusing on what *WAS* working for me in the present moment, it gave me the fortitude to embrace a new way of thinking and a new way of acting in body. I never gave up hope that my legs would fully recover in due time. I simply let go and let God work out the *details*!"

"Wow, that's an amazing story! Do you think that you could teach me how to swing a golf club like that?" I asked doubtfully.

"Absolutely!" he said enthusiastically. "But in order to fully grasp this technique for yourself, you will have to completely let go of all your past teachings and re-learn everything that you have ever been taught with an open heart and an open mind."

I nodded. He continued.

"If you are willing to do that then I will teach you not only this unusual golf swing but perhaps a few life lessons I've picked up along the way. I feel like I'm living an inspired life and would love to share a bit of my ideas on creating wholeness, peace, and health from the inside out. That is if you are willing to listen to the ramblings of a simple old man with a funny golf swing." Bob seemed sincere in his desire to become my new instructor.

"Yes – GREAT! I am ready and willing to learn! When can we start?" I asked, enthused by this opportunity.

"We can begin next Saturday, but we will need to work together once a week for an entire year in order to make progress on your golf swing -- or your life for that matter." Bob chuckled at his own suggestion. "I'm not implying that either is not up to par, but everyone always has plenty of room for improvement."

"Perfect! So how much are your teaching fees?" I asked looking at him with curiosity.

"That's a great question. My fees are *high* as it requires you to be punctual. You must be here on time, every time, no exceptions. You must not cancel a lesson except in dire circumstances," he said.

"You must be willing to listen even if you don't quite agree with me and be able to focus on the entire lesson. You must also be able to silence the inner critic after performing a bad shot. Are you willing and able to pay this price for my humble services?"

"Yes – absolutely! I'm ready!" I answered. We agreed to meet every Saturday at 1 pm sharp for twelve consecutive months. I didn't realize it at the time but that decision was about to shift my perception and the *internal* course of my life forever!

Follow Your Intuition

With the exception of those who have the misfortune of working on Saturdays, everyone will tell you that Saturdays are meant for sleeping in. Yet, there I was, sun barely shining through my window, wide awake. Anticipation will do that to you, and on this morning my anticipation skyrocketed through the roof. Look out world! Today I start taking golf lessons!

I liberated my dusty golf bag from the back of my closet, my first step toward becoming the next LPGA tour pro. Since I was up early, I polished my golf clubs. I certainly didn't want to be late, especially since this was part of my agreement with Bob that I wanted to honor.

I left my apartment at 10:30 am to gas up my car, leave extra room to navigate any unexpected traffic delays, and arrive at the golf range by 1 pm sharp! When I arrived at the range, Bob waved me over to an area under the shade where he would conduct our first lesson. Something about Bob's presence put me at ease straight away and filled me with peace. He had a certain glow and gentleness about his demeanor that warmed me immediately.

"For today's lesson we are going to work on your golf grip," Bob began. "You can choose the baseball grip, the overlapping grip, or the interlocking grip. Just choose whichever grip feels most comfortable to you and go with that." He demonstrated each grip.

"Whichever method you choose," he continued, "just be sure to hold the club with a relaxed grip. This will allow the club head to turn over when you swing through the ball, giving you better accuracy and better distance," he advised. I nodded in understanding. "The most important thing to remember in making decisions is to always trust your 'intuition' to guide you toward making the best choice," he said.

"What exactly is intuition? How can it guide me toward making good decisions?" I asked.

"God gave us intuition and discernment, which is an intuitional guidance system designed to help us find a way that resonates with our soul in making daily decisions." He leaned easily on his club as he began to explain.

"It's also known as the Holy Spirit," he smiled, "the Comforter, the Counselor, the Still Small Voice, and/or the Higher Self - the direct communication link to God that is *within* you." I'd heard similar versions of this before but hadn't given it a second thought. Bob explained it all with such ease.

"Intuition is the universal language of the soul, the one tongue we all speak, no matter what our culture, religion, race, gender or language is." He placed his club iron in the trolley and pulled out another. I didn't speak. I just waited for him to continue. "One of the best ways to tell if you are following your intuition -- your intuitional guidance system -- is by paying close attention to how you feel.

"You will always know when you are listening to your intuition because you will feel more alive, free in your spirit, and stronger inside because you are taking the advice of yourself which is the voice of God communicating within you," he explained. "If you second guess yourself, and go back to what's comfortable - your old ways of thinking based on logic - which is what you think you *should* do based on what other people think you should do - you will feel confused, fearful and sometimes even sad."

"I can relate to that," I said.

"When you let go and relax your *grip* - pardon the pun," he chuckled, and I couldn't help but laugh with him, "over what other people think, you will begin to hear the small still voice of God directing your every action instead of outside influences directing them for you." He took a few practice swings across the ground before continuing his speech.

"Your intuition will never steer you wrong and when you hear its call, you will make better decisions with better clarity and accuracy, and you will be able to go the distance in every action, word, and deed."

"Wow!!!" I said. "I had no idea that learning how to hold a golf club could teach me to make better choices. Mom and Dad always said that God lives inside me, but I never really understood what they meant or how it was relevant in my decision making process."

"If you ever find yourself confused about something or not knowing what to do, you can always pose a question to your Heart." He smiled.

"What exactly does that mean?" I asked, taken aback.

"It means trusting your intuition your own built-in intuitional guidance system for the answer. That reminds me of a story." His eyes twinkled at the thought. He seemed transported to another place as he began to tell me the story:

> *"Grandpa, what are you whispering?" The little boy asked, noticing that his grandfather was whispering something to himself before going to bed.*
>
> *"I posed a question to my Heart" Grandfather said.*
>
> *The boy was surprised. "What does that mean?"*
>
> *The wise grandfather told him, "I don't always know what I should do, so I will pose a question to my Heart and go to sleep, and in the morning my Heart will tell me what to do."*
>
> *"And where does your Heart know it from?" The boy replied.*
>
> *"The Heart knows everything. We are all learning from it all the time. And I recommend when you are looking for*

an answer to a difficult question, when something isn't clear, or you feel confused about what to do about a situation, you can try this simple practice at bedtime and the next morning the answers will become clear to you."

The grandfather finished, "Just make sure you do it with complete faith. Do this and your life will be blessed with inner peace and purpose."

Bob seemed to drift off to an old but pleasant memory. When he came back to the present moment, he picked up the club and took a few perfect swings. For the rest of our lesson, Bob and I experimented with the different golf grips to find the most natural one for me.

On my drive back home, I couldn't get the lesson out of my head. It amazed me that something as simple as a golf grip could be so helpful in explaining the power of choice and trusting in my own intuition. I believed what Bob shared with me was true because I have always felt the presence of God from *within* but didn't know how to tune in to this intuition. I had a very hard time hearing that inner voice through all the noise and commotion of my life.

> **Finding the perfect grip on a golf club is like searching and embracing the best situation in life, love, career and relationship.**

Dearest One,

In this lesson, Bob opened up my awareness and taught me about trusting my own inner guidance from within (God within). He showed me that we each have absolute freedom to choose the way we want to believe, live, and behave in the world.

Bob taught me to be *responsible* for the person I am by taking control of my own thoughts and ultimately the path I choose. When we give this responsibility away to others, we lose the power to change our life and transform our world.

I love this quote by Steve Jobs, as I can picture Bob echoing these sentiments:

"Your time is limited; don't waste it living someone else's life. Don't be trapped by dogma, which is living the result of other people's thinking. **Don't let the noise of other's opinions drown out your own inner voice.** *And most important, have the courage to follow your heart and intuition, they somehow already know what you truly want to become. Everything else is secondary."*

So many people feel like they don't have any control over situations in their lives. I felt empowered and absolutely thrilled to learn that I had the power *within* to make my own choices instead of merely following what others believed to be the right path for me. I needed to establish a mindset to cut through all the outside noises in my life, so that I could listen to my own voice (my intuition) from within.

As a young adult, I was afraid to stand up for my own beliefs. What a scary and challenging endeavor! I didn't want to be judged when I shared my views, so I often felt conflicted. I felt that in order to know what was true for me concerning God, I would have to experience God on my own terms – I couldn't accept what other people expected me to believe.

Intuitively, I always felt that faith was deeper than our learning. I believe that Faith is rooted in our being and rises up from the nature of who we *ARE*.

Faith is trusting that no matter what happens in life, good or bad, everything will work out just fine because God has our back at all times.

I witnessed this at an early age through my Mom's example when she stood up to my dad, the church, and their rules/belief system. She paid a price for standing up for what she believed in, but she remained true to herself and her own beliefs. I will never forget her courage and the lesson she taught me.

Dear God,
Lost in a world where the company you keep is few,
almost seems pointless at times.

*To give up and surrender my beliefs
would be an easy choice.
I will walk in faith,
not in fear!*

Finding Purpose

Dear God,
I ask with a pure and open heart that I find my true purpose and
fulfill my highest potential.
Thank you God.
Love, Gena

The sunshine poured brightly through my windshield as I drove to the golf course, anticipating yet another amazing lesson from Bob. I could not wait to get on the course.

"Hi, Gena! Here you are again - right on time! I just love how punctual you are!" Bob said in his strong chipper voice.

"I've been leaving my house at 10:30 am, which gives me plenty of time to get here. I really look forward to these lessons and I have the timing down now."

"Attagirl, I enjoy your enthusiasm and your eagerness to learn! So, are you ready for today's lesson?"

"I am, and I can't wait to see what you have in store for me today!"

"Funny you should say that Gena, because today's lesson requires you to see my golf swing in your mind's eye."

"What do you mean?" I asked, unsure.

"I have learned that our body copies pictures of physical motion, which occur in our subconscious mind. We don't learn a golf swing by memorizing the how-to, but rather by creating a picture in our *mind's eye* of ourselves making the proper motion. This is true for every physical movement we make, not just our golf swing," he enlightened me.

"Everything happens in the brain first. The mind controls the body, the body controls the club, and the club controls the ball (mind, body, and club). With the proper understanding, we can teach our body how to make the proper motion and produce consistent, predictable results even with our eyes closed. My job as your teacher is to create a picture in your mind, so you can teach your body to copy my swing. The mantra I often give to my students is, '*Get out of your head and into your body.*' In other words, feel your body copy the picture; do not tell your body *how* to copy the picture," Bob explained.

He went on to say, "Golf is not an eye-hand hit-the-ball game, but rather a motion game. Our swing motion is made away from the target and back to the target utilizing centripetal force for a maximum transfer of energy to the golf ball. The only other thing we need to do is to learn to execute this motion in *balance* so it can be repeated consistently, and that takes practice and persistence. Are you ready to test this out for yourself?" Bob seemed eager for my answer.

"What do you mean?" I asked, afraid of the answer.

"I mean, are you ready to hit some golf balls using your mind's eye?" Bob asked, as if repeating this would help me understand.

"Um…I'm getting a funny feeling that you want me to hit golf balls with my eyes closed or something crazy like that," I guessed.

"Bingo!" he laughed at my obvious doubt about this lesson.

"Oh Lord, help me," I prayed.

"Is that your way of asking God for some kind of divine intervention?" he asked.

"Yeah, I think I'm going to need it!" I replied. Bob made me laugh and immediately put me at ease.

"Not to worry," Bob replied. "I'm going to hit some balls with my eyes closed to demonstrate how it's done. Watch my swing carefully, and see it in your mind's eye so you can replicate the swing using a visual image."

Bob continued to give me specific instructions, "Before closing your eyes, be sure to establish your target line. You have to know where you want the ball to go before you can hit an accurate shot. Take your address position by aligning your body feet, hips and shoulders parallel to the target line. Grip the club and let your arms hang straight down; your hands will be positioned roughly under your chin. This is an athletic posture, relaxed and ready for action."

He placed a ball directly in front of him on the ground. He then closed his eyes, wound up his upper torso like a tight rubber band, and on his downswing made perfect contact with the ball as if his eyes were wide open.

Once again, I was completely taken aback by his ability to hit a perfect shot. With his eyes closed, he continued to hit ball after ball with perfect precision, unprecedented distance, and uncanny accuracy. I watched intently as I took it all in. I burned the image of his swing into my mind's eye down to the very last detail.

When it was my turn to address the ball, I aligned my body parallel with my established target line and closed my eyes. I stood over my ball and wound up my upper torso. The image of Bob's golf swing was so fresh in my mind that I could actually feel the impact of the shot in my body prior to making contact with the ball. The swing was over before I knew it. When I opened my eyes the ball was no longer in front of me. Bob just stood over me smiling like a proud papa.

Excitement rushed through my body. I learned to use the power of my mind's eye that I didn't even know existed until now. For the rest of the afternoon, I continued to hit ball after ball with my eyes closed. Bob wanted to ensure that the image of his swing was firmly impressed upon my subconscious mind.

We were exhausted and thirsty, so Bob poured some ice water from his cooler jug for us. We sat on a bench, under some shade trees, overlooking the driving range with the perfect backdrop of the rolling green hills of Napa Valley sprawled out before us like a painting.

Bob took a long drink and then asked, "Do you have any questions before we end today's lesson?"

"Yes, actually, I do," I replied.

"Well, then, swing away!" Bob gestured a golf swing with his arms.

"I know we are going to keep working on my golf swing, but I've really been doing a lot of reflecting on our conversation from our last session. Last week we talked about intuition and how I should trust it in guiding me toward making choices that are in alignment with my highest purpose. I've been trying to figure out what I was made for and my special calling ever since I was born. I've been asking God to reveal this to me as far back as I can remember, and I still don't know the answer. All week long, I practiced listening to the voice of God within me, but I still can't figure out what my calling is or why I was born. A bit deep, I know, for the end of our golf lesson," I admitted.

Bob closed his eyes and fell into a still silence. I don't know where he went during that time period, but I waited patiently for his answer and then he began to speak.

"Gena, some children of God, like yourself, are born into the fire. The fire represents difficult and challenging times directly upon their arrival into this life in order to bring a cleansing to their shadow; the shadow, I believe, represents all the unhealed emotions and negative experiences, early on in their childhood," he said, making it sound very simple.

He stretched out, then continued, "The fruit of these challenges during early childhood produces unprecedented love, compassion, and understanding toward the rest of humanity. Your parents are the gateway for bringing you into this physical realm. They are also your spiritual teachers, supporting you and bringing forth all the experiences you need to move through the challenges of daily life and into an understanding of Love in order to eventually become an instrument of that Love."

"So, what is my calling or my highest purpose?" I asked again.

"Your highest purpose is to live that Love and to share and express that Love with the rest of the world. Your highest purpose is to demonstrate that God's unconditional Love is found in the here and now, right in the center of your Heart. Heaven and Earth are the same world, and in order to experience heaven, you have to first experience your soulfulness here on earth in your golf shoes and socks as well as in your mind," Bob clarified.

It was a lot to take in!

"What does '*I have to experience my soulfulness here on earth in my golf shoes and socks*' mean?" I asked.

Bob continued, "Illumination, enlightenment, or conversion, whatever name people may give it occurs right here on earth in the midst of our ordinary daily life experiences. Every aspect of daily life, no matter how mundane, is the path to God," he explained. He moved closer to make sure I was paying attention. I could hear it in his voice how deeply moved he was that I was interested in his favorite subject.

"Our daily life experiences here on earth can express more light, more love, more openness, and more freedom if we choose to shine our light in the world. In order to authentically live your highest purpose and fully experience unconditional Love from *within* you must first get *REAL* here in this world. Getting real is taking out the garbage, getting real is shoveling the snow, getting real is driving to work every day in heavy traffic, getting real is taking care of a sick child, getting real is growing up in challenging family situations," he reiterated.

I nodded. I was pretty sure I understood exactly what he was saying.

"Getting real is being able to do all these things while still holding the blessed state of *being*. Enlightenment is the realization that there is nothing you have to do but live *consciously*. The path to enlightenment is not directed toward a fixed goal somewhere in the future it's a committed relationship to the expansion of Spirit that dwells within you and expresses itself through you within each experience and through each moment," Bob said, as he pulled out a golf club from the cart and started swinging it about. He then turned back to me and continued.

"When you live openly and genuinely from your heart, no matter what struggles you are facing, you can then move deeply into the presence of the *Divine*. Your highest purpose in the physical realm of daily life is to meet each challenge that you face with grace and integrity. This brings me to a story about encountering obstacles on your path that I want to share:

> "In ancient times, a king had a boulder placed on a roadway. Then he hid himself and watched to see if anyone would remove the huge rock. Some of the king's wealthiest merchants and courtiers came by and simply walked around it.
>
> "Many loudly blamed the king for not keeping the road clear, but none did anything about getting the big stone out of the way. Then a peasant came along carrying a load of vegetables on his back. On approaching the boulder, the peasant laid down his burden and tried to move the stone to the side of the road.
>
> "After much pushing and straining, he finally succeeded. As the peasant picked up his load of vegetables, he noticed a purse lying in the road where the boulder had been. The purse contained many gold coins and a note from the king indicating that the gold was for the person who removed the boulder from the roadway. The peasant learned what many others never understand."

It was powerful. He pressed on with his explanation and said, "Every obstacle presents an opportunity to improve one's condition. You must take on and experience each challenge fully so that you can learn from it and then move through it in the spirit of Love. Jesus' attention was always focused on God, and that is the example we should *all* imitate. Joy, fulfillment, and Heaven can be experienced right here, right now."

"Wow!!!" I was transfixed on him and the valuable lesson he spoke so passionately about. "I had no idea that my parents have been my spiritual teachers, allowing all the experiences I needed to become an instrument of Love. I never looked at their role in my life in this way before," I said.

"I have spent so much energy seeking out my purpose and reason for being and begging God for many years to reveal this to me. I always expected to receive some loud message from the clouds that would tell me what to do and why. I can begin to see now the importance of listening to my intuition, which all along has been leading me on the path. I didn't realize that all the challenges I faced as a child have been preparing me for something so beautiful."

I smiled and felt goose bumps at this breakthrough. "I do feel that I have so much love to share and very much want to do exactly that," I admitted.

"And so you will because you choose to," Bob replied. "You are still just beginning to truly understand these deeper truths, but all of your experiences have been preparing you. As time goes on you will continue to experience and pass through all the *two-sidedness* of life. These seemingly opposite polarities like good and bad, light and dark, hot and cold, but through it all you will eventually let go of the struggle and come to a complete understanding and acceptance of reality or that which just is."

"Which is what?" I asked.

"That there can be no duality, no judgment, and/or separation from God. *God loves you unconditionally, no matter what!* When you choose to live in the light of Love and compassion, you will embody this as being your reality, but you will also observe the darkness as being a *choice* of your free will as well," Bob explained.

"This is making some sense, but is a bit like a foreign language," I admitted again. "To make sure that I understand what you are saying, the good and the not-so-good happenings in my life were all learning experiences that were part of the divine plan to help me with the *desire* to improve and grow as life moves on," I said, as I paced, trying to recall his exact words and meaning before continuing. "Opposites what you call *duality,* are not really opposites. Instead, they are two sides of the same thing. Kind of like a coin; a coin has two opposite sides, but it is still just one coin."

He nodded, so I continued.

"So, I'm taking this to mean that light and dark, for example, are *both* aspects of God, which means that there is only one *single* Source for all that is!"

"Our intuition leads us to express and experience whatever we need in any moment; on one occasion it might recommend an action which we could deem as *generous*, and on another occasion it might recommend an action which we could deem as *non-generous*. So, just say, if, for example, we want to experience more peace in our life then we should also acknowledge the reality of conflict because what we resist persists, so to speak," I revealed.

"Wow. Yes." He nodded his approval.

"When we encounter negative circumstances or difficult situations, we see them for what they are, but we don't allow them to affect our well-being," I said emphatically.

"That's exactly right, Gena! Life's challenges make us stronger, and in turn enable us to help others going through the same situation as an instrument of Love. Difficult times are part of life—they are like storms. We need to learn how to prepare and ride them out with grace and integrity. This brings me to another story about the pencil and the Pencil Maker," Bob smiled, as he began his tale:

> *The Pencil Maker took the pencil aside, just before putting him into the box.*
>
> *"There are 5 things you need to know," he told the pencil, "before I send you out into the world; always remember them and never forget, and you will become the best pencil you can be.*
>
> *"One: You will be able to do many great things, but only if you allow yourself to be held in someone's hand.*

"Two: You will experience a painful sharpening from time to time, but you'll need it to become a better pencil.

"Three: You will be able to correct any mistake you might make.

"Four: The most important part of you will always be what's inside.

"And Five: On every surface you are used on, you must leave your mark. No matter what the condition, you must continue to write."

The pencil understood and promised to remember, and went into the box with purpose in its heart.

"Now, let's replace the pencil with you." Bob continued.

"Gena, you will be able to do many great things, but only if you allow yourself to be held in God's hand and allow other human beings to access you for the many gifts you possess. You will experience a painful sharpening from time to time by going through various problems in life, but you'll need it to become a stronger person. You will be able to correct any mistakes you might make. The most important part of you will always be what's on the inside. On every surface you walk through, you must leave your mark. No matter what the situation, you must continue to live your highest purpose," Bob insisted.

"I just love this analogy – this makes so much sense to me now. Can I ask another question about weakness?" I said, pursuing more answers.

"Swing away…" Bob touched the golf club he was leaning on.

"If my highest purpose is to become an instrument of Love, will other people see this as a weakness and try to take advantage of me?" I asked.

"This is a great question, Gena, and the answer is *NO*, not if you establish clear and healthy boundaries that honor yourself and others. When defining your boundaries you must respect both others and yourself," Bob replied.

"What are boundaries?" I questioned.

"Guidelines that you create that are reasonable and permissible ways for other people to behave around you and how you will respond when someone steps outside those limits. When you don't have clear and healthy boundaries set in place, other people will take advantage of you and step over the line without even realizing it; and respecting other people's boundaries helps make you a more desirable person to be around," Bob explained.

"How do I go about establishing healthy boundaries that honor myself and others at the same time?" I probed again.

"When you identify the need to set a boundary, do it clearly, preferably without anger, and in as few words as possible. Do not justify, apologize for, or rationalize the boundary you are setting. Do not argue. Just set the boundary calmly, firmly, clearly and respectfully.

"When you stand up for yourself, you gain a sense of empowerment and a higher level of self-worth. This provides an opportunity for those around you to do the same, and you will create beautiful relationships that nourish, respect, and support you," Bob replied.

"Thank you, Bob. I'm beginning to understand a lot of things that have puzzled me for years. I'm so grateful to have someone to talk to about things that really matter. Well, we better get to work on this swing of mine before our time is up!" I said, moving toward the green.

"Perfect! Let's move forward then."

Dearest One,

I didn't realize that God's love was found in the here and now in everyday life and all its messy glory. I learned from Bob that God's love is expressed in us, through us, and all around us! God's love is experienced in a sunset, a wildflower, and a baby's laugh because how else can any of these things exist without our Creator? I thought I could only find Gods love in Heaven, and only if I was lucky enough to make it there.

I thought Heaven was a place that only *chosen* people could attain. I didn't realize that simply being an expression, an Instrument of God's Love, *WAS* the path to God and Heaven and to my own happiness and well-being.

This insight *ROCKED* my world! The feeling was surreal. It was as if I entered Heaven the very moment Bob shared this revelation with me. I felt God's energy reach in and hug my heart for the very first time. I felt connected to all that IS and ever has been! I felt completely *JOYFUL*! I've never experienced such happiness in my mind, body, and spirit until that moment. I felt grounded and fully alive, right here on earth, in my golf shoes and socks.

I was very grateful in that moment for my early childhood challenges and for my parents' role in my life. For a long time, I held on to feelings of frustration, resentment, anxiety, and confusion for being born into the midst of my parents' war, but I learned from Bob that God, The Living Spirit, knew me and had plans for me even before I was conceived. I discovered my greatest purpose is to *BE* the Living Expression of God's Love.

This made me so happy! God (my inner voice) revealed a new world to me. I was given a new perception a completely new and exhilarating insight. All of the loveless, negative thoughts and feelings were being transformed into a more positive and loving light.

I felt as if all my fearful/painful childhood emotions and feelings were the boulder that God was waiting for me to remove from the roadway (of my consciousness). The golden coins and the reward in Bob's story were the feelings of pure love and peace from within. In other words, once I finally let go of my resistance to experiencing the energy of God's Love this presence could enter my Mind and my Heart-space. I was beginning to understand this is what Heaven on Earth means in the here and *NOW*.

I felt the presence of the Divine!

Dear God,
The Greatest Movement is already here right now.
The Greatest Movement is and always will be Love.
It is our greatest offering to "Become" Love.
There is only one true religion —
to know our innermost being.

Focus and Silence

Dear God,
I am still.
Let the earth be still
along with me.

On the way to the golf course, my excitement and anticipation rose over the thought of another fascinating golf lesson. Bob's lessons inspired and motivated me to stand up for myself in this world. I arrived at the golf course eager to continue this intriguing new journey of self-discovery. I enjoyed the golf, but it was the discussions I shared with Bob that started me on the path to deeper thinking. I spotted Bob in his bright green sweater and rushed up to greet him.

He smiled and looked as happy to see me as I was to get to spend more time with him. He immediately got down to business. "For today's lesson we are going to talk about applying one-pointed attention to your swing, which can also be applied in daily life." Bob swung his club as he began to tell me about my next lesson.

"Golf is a game that requires intense concentration and focus," he said. "The golf swing is a mechanical process, and you will find greater success with your swing if you apply laser focused attention to every shot. I will show you the basic mechanics, and then you will work on repeating these basics the same way for each swing," he explained.

"Great!" I said excitedly.

"As you become proficient in executing the basics, you can then start to experiment with subtle changes to your swing that can change the flight of the ball to match your shot needs. You must first learn to be attentive and be able to focus your thoughts on one thing at a time," he clarified.

"I can do that." I smiled.

"Your sense of well-being is decreased when you have scattered focus." He continued. "In addition, if you become overburdened by too many details, it is much harder to be present in the moment. Slowing down and concentrating on one thing at a time will provide the space you need to respond to stress, rather than merely *reacting* to it." He swung his club around as if to demonstrate; it was methodical, hypnotic, as if he was completely in tune with it.

"From now on I would like you to consider your golf swing as a form of mindful-meditation in order to cultivate this single-pointed focus. Anything you do in daily life with your *full attention* is a means to quiet your mind in order to give birth to the *BEST* that's within you."

"I don't know too much about meditation, but I occasionally watch Bruce Lee movies where he sits cross legged in a lotus position and breathes funny. Is that what you mean by mindful-meditation?" I joked.

Bob chuckled at my worldly innocence. "I certainly don't expect you to meditate in a lotus position on the golf course, but it is a good idea to focus attention on your breathing just before you prepare for a shot. If other thoughts come to mind, let them pass and refocus on the rhythm of your breathing. You can even use this simple golf-specific affirmation to quiet your mind while you focus on your shot, which is: *see it, feel it and do it*."

He continued, "If other thoughts come to mind, let them pass and immediately focus back on your affirmation. A quiet, non-analytical mind is necessary to get into the flow and become immersed in the execution of your swing. In order to quiet your mind, don't ruminate about past shots or holes and let them obstruct your thinking. Be totally focused on the shot you have *NOW*, not the one you had ten minutes ago."

"When applying mindful meditation, you are simply focusing your thought on one specific thing. You are focusing on the moment, the *now*, and nothing else. You are not thinking about the past, or the future. You are not thinking about the bills you have to pay, or what you are going to have for dinner, or what you are going to wear to work tomorrow. You are only paying attention to the task at hand right *NOW*." Bob paused and then continued his discourse.

"It may not sound all that difficult, but training your mind to only focus on the moment you're experiencing requires a lot of practice. A pro golfer who consistently sinks his putts has the ability to do this. I'm not saying all pro golfers are meditation gurus. Some people are just naturally better at focusing than others. But if you find yourself feeling distracted on the golf course, or maybe you don't feel distracted but your game just isn't as good as you'd like it to be, mindful meditation is just the kind of practice and training you need.

"The secret in executing a successful golf shot and/or living a happy life is quieting your mind and doing one thing at a time with full attention. That sounds simple, but it's not so easy. This is because our mind tends to flit off into all kinds of other directions. We start to think about what happened to a friend we loved five years ago, or thinking about work, or even planning our next vacation. When we do that, we miss out on the happy moments in the here and now."

"I'm not sure I follow or understand how we miss out on happiness?" I asked.

"Because when our minds are focused on other things we miss out on the moment. Most people don't realize it, but what truly makes us happy is experiencing the moment. Very often, we are surrounded with noise all day long, and we keep moving from one task to the other without taking a break to think, to reflect, to introspect. But for all these things, we require silence and appreciation for the moment.

"I seek silence several times every day and cannot imagine what it would be like never to experience this peace and quiet and all the benefits it brings me. Silence refreshes my soul and heals me of the exhaustion and angst caused by the noise of everyday life. Silence provides me with the spaciousness in which my many scattered parts can come together and mend.

This brings me to a story about a farmer and his missing watch. That is, if you don't mind listening to my ramblings." I had come to love Bob's stories by this point.

> *There once was a farmer who discovered that he had lost his watch in the barn. It was no ordinary watch because it had sentimental value for him.*
>
> *After searching high and low for a long while, he gave up and enlisted the help of a group of children playing outside the barn. He promised them that the person who found it would be rewarded.*
>
> *Hearing this, the children hurried inside the barn, went through and around the entire stack of hay but still could not find the watch. Just when the farmer was about to give up looking for his watch, a little boy went up to him and asked to be given another chance.*
>
> *The farmer looked at him and thought, "Why not? After all, this kid looks sincere enough." So the farmer sent the little boy back in the barn. After a while the little boy came out with the watch in his hand! The farmer was both happy and surprised, and so he asked the boy how he succeeded where the rest had failed.*

> *The boy replied, "I did nothing but sit on the ground and listen. In the silence, I heard the ticking of the watch and just looked for it in that direction."*

"I love this story, Bob, and I think I am slowly beginning to catch on. What I'm hearing you say is that a peaceful mind can think better than a worked up mind. So we should allow a few minutes of silence to enter our mind every day. We will always know exactly what to do when we simply silence our mind and let our intuition guide us in all areas of our life."

"That's exactly it, Gena! It's a simple, yet practical approach for happy and joyful living."

Dearest One,

As Bob shared his wisdom on the importance of being focused, quieting the mind, and learning the various mechanics of the golf swing, I found myself hanging on to every word. Bob's peaceful disposition and kind spirit touched my heart and inspired me on so many levels. Staying focused can help you accomplish almost anything you desire. Mastering focused attention will make you a better listener, super charge your professional life, and allow you to come up with quicker solutions to solve life's challenges.

In this lesson, Bob taught me how to focus my attention in the present moment and assess whether my field of attention fit my purpose. He made it clear that sometimes you have to shut out the rest of the world in order to rid your mind of useless distractions to achieve your goals and dreams.

We only have so much mental energy. If day-to-day affairs are weighing you down, bothering you, creating anxiety, and making you insecure, it's draining a lot of that valuable time and energy that could be spent achieving greatness by applying focused attention.

With focused attention, you can slow yourself down in order to become *less reactive* to outside situations. Reactive people are like characters in a movie, playing out the script. They sometimes resemble powerless *victims*, their lives being run by external factors. They have little control over their emotions. Instead their emotions are dictated by someone or something else, by circumstances and the outside environment.

> **Focused attention is essentially a practice of mindfulness.**

I love this quote by Stephen Covey:

> *"Reactive people are often affected by their physical environment. If the weather is good, they feel good. If it isn't, it affects their attitude and performance. Proactive people carry their own weather with them."*

During this session, I began to see Bob as a spiritual teacher supporting my journey in the same way that he explained my parents' role in this undertaking. I had prayed that God would help me find deeper meaning and purpose in my life, and I received my answer through Bob, who was just an ordinary man with an extraordinary golf swing.

It certainly is true that coming to understand the deeper realities and enlightenment occurs right here on earth in our golf shoes and socks in all our ordinary real life stuff.

I began to understand that our ordinary human life is truly extraordinary when we align our mind with the presence and energy of God's Love. I also tuned in to the fact that in order to hear Gods voice from within, I had to silence my mind and thoughts.

At that time in my life, I didn't realize that God spoke to me in my everyday life, through daily circumstances, people, and events.

> **Daily life is a living prayer—**
> **a daily conversation with God.**

Bob taught me that when my mind is quiet, I can hear God in everything. In the animals, in a baby's cry, in a friend who needs me, in the bird's song, and in the opening of a fresh wildflower on a spring day. God's essence is that which can be found in *ALL* of creation, from the magnificence of the oceans to the canyons and deserts to the extraordinary and infinite array of all living things. God's essence *IS* what makes every facet of everyday life a prayer and a song.

I sensed God's presence at the park with my mom when I was only seven years old, but I had forgotten what God's Love felt like. I knew as a child that God's church wasn't simply a building where people wore suits and sang hymns – God's Church was found in the living *BODY* of all of God's creation.

I learned that to be a *BODY*, each individual part contributes to the other parts. For example, every cell in our body requires oxygen, but it is the mouth and the lungs that inhale it and process it. Similarly, every part of the body needs or wants to eat, drink, think, talk, walk, dance, plant a garden, and watch a sunset. Certain tissues, organs, and limbs assume the task and do it for every other part.

A body is more than a physical object. It is a *spiritual* idea the concept that an action by one of the collective parts is, in essence, an action of the *whole*.

Prior to Bob's teachings, I also didn't realize that my intuition was God's voice directing my every move. I always sensed this, but I didn't know how to fully connect with my inner-guidance. I began to sense that God made all living things in his/her own image, not in shape, not in intelligence, not in eyes, not in hands or feet, but in his/her total *inwardness*. In here, is the image of God.

God is found within!

I realized that listening to God from within my own being was just like listening to anyone in regular conversation, but before I could truly hear, I had to be ready to fully listen. Just as in a conversation, I cannot really hear the other person if I'm talking, or if my mind is distracted. So it is with God. If I want to hear God speak from within, I have to be quiet, and I have to be completely focused on what he/she is saying. This is what Bob taught me through his lesson and through his story of the farmer and his missing watch.

> **Listening to God requires deliberate choice**
> **to shut out the chaos around me**
> **and focus my thoughts**
> **on Gods promptings to lead the way!**

Dear God,

I am thankful for my stillness.
I sit in quite thought.
Love stills my heart.
Love speaks
to those who are stilled.
I am grateful
to deliver this message.
Let stillness speak.
Feel Love's silence.
May your heart
be touched
by the stillness
of your own
Whisper.

CHAPTER 6

Choose Happiness

The sun played peek-a-boo with the clouds as I drove to the golf course for my next lesson with Bob. Driving along the highway, I bounced back and forth between feeling content with my life to feeling overwhelming frustration. At times, I struggled with feeling content for so many blessings in my life, but then my intellectual judgment would enter the picture followed by a stressed out feeling. Perhaps this is why children are typically happy until their intellectual powers step in, judging good from bad. It seems we are trained to hold onto these concepts as our emotional and mental stresses begin to emerge. I realized reaching my full potential is what would make me feel content inside.

"Bob, I've been reflecting on all you said last week, and your teachings are so practical and make so much sense, but I still struggle to find happiness and contentment from within. Here's a good example, I'm so grateful for my job and the security it provides, but I want to become more than a Sales Support Specialist," I said.

"I want to work with computers as a Systems Analyst, but I don't have the schooling or background that it takes to even apply for the position. I suppose I'll never be smart enough or good enough to ever achieve that level of success within my company. How can I possibly be someone with a higher call if I can't even advance within my own company?

"I feel like such a failure especially when I compare myself to others who are smarter, more educated, and more successful than me. I should be so much more, but I don't ever see that happening. Not in my lifetime anyway." Bob took a big drink from his water jug before addressing my question. I had a strange feeling that I just opened up a big can of worms with this topic.

"I can definitely feel your frustration today Gena, but being in tune with your higher calling and becoming an instrument of love has nothing to do with your current job title or position. It's about having a good attitude and being grateful for your present situation no matter what. An instrument of love embodies a state of internal peace that persists no matter what is lacking in your life, or what might be happening around you. When you become an instrument of love, you have a deep sense of joy and contentment that cannot be destroyed by any external factors or forces," he said.

"We all have a tendency to compare ourselves to others, but as you can see, this only makes us unhappy. Comparing yourself to people who are higher up on the corporate ladder won't get you ahead in your company. Instead, look to your peers for inspiration. Look to these people to motivate you, to make you a better *YOU*. Don't look at them and beat yourself up or become envious. Life puts us down enough, and we need to be our own heroes.

If you really want something bad enough then work for it! Don't allow something as small as a college degree stand in your way of greatness. Put a smile on your face, even if your heart is discouraged, and with that attitude, life will open up what seems like miraculous opportunities and everything will fall into place. Now back to the task at hand. Let's talk about creating a state of happiness both on the course and off the course." Bob smiled, as we had covered a lot of important ground already.

"All success in life is the product of proper mental preparedness. The same is true in the game of golf. Each time you address your ball, be aware of your mental attitude and level of enjoyment. For example, are you still mad about the previous shot? If so, take a deep breath and gather your thoughts.

"Stay in the present moment, and just be thankful that you are given this wonderful opportunity to play golf on this beautiful day. An attitude check before each shot will have you feeling more relaxed and gives you the chance to play your very best.

"Golf is a game of ecstasy, or it's a game of agony, and we have to learn to take the good with the bad. Golf mimics daily life with its ups and downs and success and failures, but in order to create a state of happiness, you have to develop and strengthen your inner-resolve so that no bad shot, trial, or hardship can ever destroy your peace of mind.

"Most people aren't happy because they reject the present moment, which is what is going on in their lives *right now*. They do this by groaning, getting upset, and wishing they were either someone else or somewhere else. They continually wish their time away or feel down about a situation. In other words, they are unconsciously rejecting what has already occurred.

"This brings me to a story about two travelers and the farmer." Bob changed into his story-telling voice:

> *A traveler came upon an old farmer hoeing in his field beside the road. Eager to rest his feet, the wanderer hailed the countryman, who seemed happy enough to straighten his back and talk for a moment.*
>
> *"What sort of people live in the next town?" asked the stranger.*
>
> *"What were the people like where you've come from?" replied the farmer, answering the question with another question.*
>
> *"They were a bad lot. Troublemakers, all of them, and lazy too. They are the most selfish people in the world, and not one of them is to be trusted. I'm happy to be leaving the scoundrels."*
>
> *"Is that so?" replied the old farmer. "Well, I'm afraid that you'll find the same sort in the next town. Disappointed, the traveler trudged on his way, and the farmer returned to his work.*
>
> *Sometime later another stranger, coming from the same direction, hailed the farmer, and they stopped to talk.*

"What sort of people live in the next town?" he asked.

"What were the people like where you've come from?" replied the farmer once again.

"They were the best people in the world. Hard-working, honest, and friendly. I'm sorry to be leaving them."

"Fear not," said the farmer. "You'll find the same sort in the next town."

Bob went back to his point. "The key to achieving happiness is increasing your thought pattern by practicing being present in the moment and learning to accept whatever comes across your path, without reacting negatively to it. If you can get the *SWING* of this (excuse the pun again), it is far more effective than other options. What do you think would happen if you woke up one morning and fully accepted the weather as it is, and didn't allow it to influence your state of mind or well-being by resisting it internally?" Bob asked me intently.

"I would feel a sense of freedom and aliveness! I would enjoy the day no matter what the weather," I exclaimed with a smile on my face.

"Exactly! What would happen to you if any trivial incident, out of your immediate control, didn't have the power to control your life?" Bob asked.

"I wouldn't feel victimized by my outside circumstances, and I would be free to live in the service of Love," I said, proud to realize this insight.

"Yes, Gena! You're catching on so fast -- you're really getting it!" Bob replied. "Fully accepting what *is* brings you not only peace of mind, but also a sense of well-being and a deep feeling of aliveness from within. Strangely enough, when you stop resisting life, life tends to respond by making your external situations better anyway."

"Yeah. I can see what you mean," I replied. "What I'm hearing you say is that waiting for something to happen or change in order to be happy is putting life on permanent hold; it's not what happens to us that's important, but how we react and handle whatever happens to us that really matters.

"When we adopt a positive attitude and are grateful for what already *is* then life becomes so much more rewarding and fulfilling instead of just something we simply endure," I revealed.

"Well said, Gena! Bravo!" Bob said in a proud manner.

"Thank you!" I said.

"It was The Dalai Lama who said, '*Happiness is not something ready-made. It comes from your own actions*,'" Bob replied.

"I'll admit I don't know who the Dalai Lama is but this makes total sense to me now. For a long time, I didn't feel that I deserved to be happy because of my sinful nature. I guess I just never felt *worthy* enough to be happy," I admitted in a somewhat sad tone.

"What do you mean by your sinful nature?" Bob asked, furrowing his brow.

"Well, I was told that we are all sinful in nature and that we need to be forgiven before we can be happy and go to heaven. I'm not sure if God has forgiven me yet. I've asked for forgiveness many times, but I'm not sure if he's heard me," I replied.

"Actually, there is no sinful nature according to God—The Living Spirit," Bob said.

"There's not?" I asked, caught off guard.

Bob continued. "No, because God - The Living Spirit doesn't *judge* you in the first place, so there is nothing to forgive. Your being is created by God – The Living Spirit, so nothing can threaten it; therefore, judgment is not necessary. This is the *GRACE* of God. Remembering this and accepting this fact is our salvation. The only ones who judge each other for their *sinful nature* are human beings.

> ***"Sinfulness is a byproduct of negative thinking which can't be a product of God.***

"We are the 'eternal and perfect nature' of God—The Living Spirit. Jesus (Yeshua[1]) knew this, and this was his teaching, but the people of his time were not ready to hear it. They could not look upon Him and recognize their own eternal and perfect

---

[1] *Yeshua is a name that means 'God is salvation' in Hebrew. Who is Yeshua? Yeshua is the same as Jesus Christ of the New Testament Bible, and the same as the Messiah which was prophesied to come through the Jewish people over and again in the Old Testament Bible, known as the Tanakh to the Jews. yeshua.org*

nature, and therefore, could not accept that their sins or wrongdoings were already forgiven through our Father's Grace.

"Instead, they needed a sacrifice of forgiveness, and so God and Jesus, being of One Spirit and Mind, compassionately allowed this to happen in order to satisfy the current level of understanding.

"Our Father and Jesus are of the same coin like we talked about in our earlier lesson. We are all sons and daughters of God - The Living Spirit. Jesus was a physical being just like you and me. He is also a spiritual being just like you and me. God's children encompass the whole of God's eternal and perfect nature. Jesus's Highest Purpose was to *BE* the Love and the Embodiment that God *IS*.

"God's Grace, unconditional love for us -- is a divine gift of the spirit. It's a free gift for you, to be you, just the way you are. There is no judgment. Judgment robs your peace of mind and zaps your energy. And inevitably, your judgment rebounds into yourself. Through God's *Grace* we are loved unconditionally no matter what we do in this lifetime, good or bad.

"When you become *self-accepting* by coming to terms with your entire self both your good and bad aspects you create a sense of balance by:

- Magnifying the positive aspects of yourself while minimizing the negative

- Not beating yourself up for mistakes; instead you learn from them and make amends when necessary

- You live each moment in the light of love and gratitude

- You know that you don't have to be perfect to live up to anyone's standards so you can laugh at yourself and not take yourself too seriously

- You have fun with life, friends, and yourself"

Bob hesitated and looked at me with genuine approval. "Gena, you are fully *worthy* in God's eyes, and you are fully loved and supported just the way you are. You are a child of God, *the eternal and perfect nature* of The Living Spirit, the miracle, the way and the light!"

"Thank you so very much, Bob," I said respectfully. I dried my tears on my shirtsleeve. For the very first time in my life, I felt an uncontrollable wave of emotion coursing throughout my body. "I never really knew until now how much God loves me unconditionally through the gift of Grace. If humans are the only ones who judge then I've been judging myself all this time. It's been me who hasn't forgiven others or myself for past mistakes. I've been holding on to feelings of resentment, anger, and frustration from *within* my own being. I can see now that mistakes are necessary for our learning experience regardless of their negative consequences."

Making mistakes is all part of the human experience, and there is "no way that we are going to escape making mistakes. We learn from our mistakes. The key is to realize our error, figure out what not to do or what to do next time we act, and move forward in the spirit of Love with that knowledge." I realized I sounded a lot like Bob, and since he was nodding his head in agreement, I went on.

"Mistakes lead us to wisdom as long as we don't repeat the same mistakes over and over again," I told him. "God loves me for who I am right now, so I will focus on Love and let the rest go. I love myself in the same way that God loves me. I love others in the same way that God loves me. I am happy and worthy and free to be me!" I surprised myself with these profound affirmations, and they resonated within me. The truth of them surrounded and embraced me.

"Beautifully said, Gena. I knew that you had the truth within you," Bob complimented. "When you are genuinely happy on the inside, you will never be defeated by trials and challenges; you will embrace them as opportunities to grow and evolve. When you have internal happiness, just being alive is the true source of joy and pleasure. Happiness is not found in things like the perfect relationship, the perfect house, the perfect body and/or the approval of other people. Happiness is found by co-creating with God by extending our Love to others.

"Co-creating with God-The Living Spirit—happens naturally whenever your soul or inner knowing inspires you to take action and follow your passion to pursue your life purpose."

"I have another question," I asked tentatively. "It's about Heaven and Hell."

"Swing away!" Bob always uses his arms to gesture a golf swing when he uses this phrase.

"Is Heaven a place of happiness and Hell a place of sadness that we go to after we die?"

"Heaven and Hell are largely in our mind," he said. "When you entertain positive thoughts, you are experiencing a state of Heaven from *within* your Heart. When you entertain negative thoughts, then your experiences will not be as pleasant, happy or joyful. Heaven and Hell can be experienced every day right here, right now depending on your outlook. We don't have to wait for death of the body to find Heaven or Hell. Both of them are within us in our daily life, in our daily attitude and in our daily conduct. If you are open, soulful, and surrendered, you are in a position to remain in Heaven in this very life on earth."

"What does surrender mean in this context?" I asked intently.

"Surrender means to always feel the Love, *The Kingdom of God*, in your Heart and to keep that as your primary focus," Bob explained. "This brings me to a story about a loving king whose Love was so *pure* that the experience of hell could not enter his mind even after his physical body died here on earth:

> *There once lived a great king who devoted his entire reign to improving the welfare of his people, and they came to love and revere him more as a saint than as a king.*

When he died, it is said, an angel came to escort him to Heaven. But the king had an unusual request.

"Before I enter eternal bliss," he asked, "May I see the suffering of those in hell?"

The angel was a bit surprised, but he agreed and let the king into another realm. What the king saw there puzzled him. Wherever he walked, he saw only happy faces.

People ran to greet him and receive his blessing; there were tears in their eyes, but they were tears of joy.

A little taken aback, the king turned to his guide and asked, "Why have you brought me here directly? I want to visit the other place first."

"Your majesty," the angel replied respectfully, "this is the other place."

"I don't understand. I expected hell to be full of suffering."

"This world is full of suffering—behind you, beyond you, wherever you cannot see. It is being near you that fills these people with joy."

"Then," said the king, "I need go no further. I have found my Heaven."

"That is such a beautiful story," I told him. "I can see that the people really loved being around the king because of his positive and loving energy that remained with him even after his physical body died."

"Absolutely, and this brings me to the subject of friendship." Bob said. "But let's save that one for next time."

Dearest One,

Daily life is filled with ups and downs, challenges, and hardships, but we don't gain anything by becoming despondent, negative, and unhappy. Displaying an optimistic attitude will not make hardships magically disappear, but we are in a better state of mind and have better control over our *reactions* and our *behaviors* when we look to the positive side. In this state of mind, we are in a better position to improve our situation. We can choose to dwell on our problems and suffer, or we can choose to focus on *solutions* and refuse to allow negative circumstances to affect our well-being.

> **Positive thinking means to be hopeful,
> and hope brings light to our shadow.**

Bob showed me that we don't need to be better than anyone else; we just need to love where we are and who we are in the moment. Instead of comparing ourselves to others, we must be grateful for the goodness that is right in front of us.

I love this quote by Neale Donald Walsch:

> *"Happiness is always found in the moment that is here, now. Constantly remembering bad things, or sad things, can rob you of your present – that is, your pre-sent – joy. Happiness has been sent to you in advance by God. It is here, in this moment, if you will seize it – and share it."*

I had never heard that sin couldn't exist in the Mind of God. I always thought God was judging me for my sinful nature. This insight threw me into a tailspin, of sorts. I thought we were all born into this world as sinners and had to ask Jesus for forgiveness plus follow all the biblical rules to enter Heaven. I grew up hearing and believing that if you weren't a Christian you were doomed and would not be spared from God's eternal wrath and judgment.

I had no idea that Jesus' teachings were simply to inform us that we are all perfect beings, just as we *ARE* in the presence of God's Love. We are all *ONE-BODY* with God; it doesn't matter what race, ethnicity, or religion there is no separation in the Mind of God. We are all born of the same *cloth*, and are all here to BE living expressions of God's Love. When I came to this understanding, I was saved in my *thinking*. My thoughts transformed from fear and judgment to love and acceptance.

> ***Being saved is a spiritual idea,***
> ***which means to be renewed of our conflicted***
> ***thinking and/or our internal struggle.***

We are born by *GRACE* to *BE* the living expressions of God's Love just like a wildflower, a bumblebee, a river and a rainbow are all perfect expressions of God's Love!

I saw that our perception of God is formed by what we have been taught, what we have read and/or experienced through other people. We forget that God is not a man/woman. Personality and characteristics apply only to physical man/woman, not to spirit.

God IS spirit, and therefore an image of our Creator has to be a spiritual image. The spiritual image of God comes to us in the example of Christ and his teachings. When we are born into a new consciousness (mind) above our human thinking, we are a *NEW* creation in God a spiritual creation. Instead of bringing God down to our human level of thinking, we *ascend* upward into the Mind of our Creator. We are all born to ascend in consciousness when we choose to align our thoughts with God's Love! If we think we are separate from God's Love and one another, we deny ourselves the experience of Happiness and Heaven on Earth right here.

This new teaching released all feelings of fear, insecurity, anxiety, and self-doubt from my being. I felt completely accepted in the eyes and energy of Gods' Love. I also felt free to love and accept others, just as they *ARE* and not to judge them for what they are *NOT*. For the very first time in my life my heart opened, and I accepted the Christ *within* me. I chose happiness.

Dear God,
I give thanks for the opportunities created by the unexpected happenings in my life and I extend my joy and happiness to ALL beings!

Friendship – Surround Yourself with Positive People

The morning was cold, but the sun was shining. Saturdays were now my new favorite day of the week, and I was especially eager to meet with Bob today. Before heading out of town, I decided to stop at our local coffee shop and grab a cup of cappuccino for my long drive ahead. Unfortunately, I unexpectedly ran into one of my co-workers.

Beth is naturally one of those negative people who continually brings drama into the workplace and pollutes the atmosphere with her toxic behavior. I certainly didn't want to spend the first part of my morning catching her negative vibe, so I tried to avoid her, but she noticed me right away as I walked into the shop.

As I was waiting in line for my cappuccino, Beth decided to fill me in on all the latest rumors at work. I swear that girl works overtime in the Gossip Department. The barista couldn't make my drink fast enough in order for me to escape the latest scandal according to Beth. The only thought that entertained my mind was all the rumors she must also be spreading about me. She talks about everyone behind their backs. Once I got my coffee, I made a mad dash to the sanctuary of my car. You know you're in bad company when your car seat is more appealing than a certain individual.

When I arrived at the golf course, I saw Bob on the range, and immediately ran over to join him.

"Hi Bob," I said eagerly. "I remember that last week you said we were going to talk about friendship today and actually the timing of that is perfect. I work with a woman who is degrading everyone around her. I actually ran into her this morning at the coffee shop, and she continued on her rampage even outside of work," I explained in a concerned manner.

"I'm really having a hard time being her friend. I don't like it when she gossips and makes up rumors and lies about other people and then acts as sweet as pie to their faces. She constantly talks trash about various co-workers and then gets upset if I don't engage and/or agree with her. I'm trying to get along with her and be her friend, but working alongside her is very difficult and brings lots of negative energy into the office. I feel really uncomfortable being around her, and I don't trust her. How do I deal with this person and still remain friendly?"

"Whoa! Slow down my little friend and catch your breath for a moment. I can see she has really gotten under your skin," Bob said. "By the way, where are your golf clubs?"

"Oh, my gosh! I left them in the trunk of my car," I said blushing.

"Well, you better go retrieve them because it's going to be really hard to hit your ball today without them." Bob giggled under his breath.

I laughed at myself and also felt a little embarrassed for my flighty temperament. I immediately ran back to my car and retrieved my clubs from the trunk. When I arrived back at the range, Bob was taking some practice shots and whistling some old familiar song like he didn't have a care in the world.

"Sorry about that Bob," I said interrupting his swing. "I guess I'm a little distracted today. I was thinking about my co-worker during the entire drive down here this morning and I guess I just needed to vent. I'm really upset about this and I just don't know how to handle her."

"Let's sit down for a spell and talk about this before we hit the links today. I can see that you're upset. Let's clear the air," Bob said with a compassionate and sincere tone.

"In the workplace, Gena, you are going to encounter negative people from time to time.

"The very best strategy when dealing with negative people is just to stay cool and deny them the satisfaction of getting you riled up or involved in their games of gossip and manipulation. When these people, like your fellow co-worker, try to lure you into a conversation that tears someone down, simply shift the energy by saying something positive about the person they are pre-judging," Bob said.

He went on to say, "At all times be honest and ethical in all of your interactions without lowering yourself to their level, and people will begin to follow suit and respect you for it. It's amazing how many more friends you will make when you follow this model and allow yourself to form your own impression of the people you meet along life's journey. The key to attracting positive uplifting friends and influences into your life always begins with *YOU!*"

"Me?"

"Yes, you," he said emphatically. "You are like a magnetic force, Gena. At every moment you are attracting what you put out into the world. Do you think anyone really wants to be around you if you are always miserable, talking trash about other people or taking out your problems on the world?" Bob smiled at me and said, "Think how hard you try to avoid this Beth character."

"That's so true. I know there are very few people who want to be in her presence. I don't like it when other people do this around me either. I have a hard time being around Beth," I said.

"Exactly! You see, Gena, when people act this way it's because they are not happy with themselves. When they are not happy with themselves they won't be happy with others either. We can be a positive example that people like Beth are looking for in order to help them shift their perception and feel better about themselves. This is what being an instrument of love is all about," Bob explained.

"Nobody is all positive or all negative, but there are people you just tend to feel more positive around. When choosing your friends, remember to use this as your barometer because other people are deciding whether they want to be around you in this same way.

"Be sure to seek out friends who are *action-oriented* and *service-oriented*. As you spend more and more time in the company of people who have these traits, you, too, will develop the same successful characteristics and put them to use in your daily life. True friends won't judge you. They may not always agree with everything you say and do, but they won't think less of you for believing differently.

"Our differences are what make great friendships! It would be very boring if we all thought alike all the time, don't you think?" Bob asked.

"I most certainly do!" I said.

"Take the game of golf, for example. As much as the sport is a physical one, it's also a social game too. You play with other people and sometimes in a friendly spirit, sometimes in a competitive one, usually in some kind of balance between the two," Bob explained. "On a beautiful day, a golf course can provide an incredibly enjoyable atmosphere of camaraderie fueled by a similar interest and a sense of feeling lucky just to be out in the fresh air. Friends will come and go in your life, Gena, but more important than how long a friendship lasts, is that a good friend will love and accept you for who you are. Now on that note, let's gather up our gear and hit the links. I'm anxious to see how your swing is evolving this week."

Dearest One,

After listening to Bob, I understood that everything we do or say has the potential to affect another individual. Bob helped me to realize that I may not have the power to change Beth, but I certainly have the power to be a positive influence in her life through my own actions and reactions.

If I take a few moments to consider how my various modes of being affect the people I spend time with each day, I come one step closer to seeing myself through their eyes. Though I may never know the impact I have made upon another human being or the scope of my influence, accepting and understanding that my attitude and choices will affect others will remind me to conduct myself with grace and integrity at all times.

When I intend to always be friendly, helpful, and responsive, I am able to attract an aura around myself that is both uplifting and inspiring. Bob helped me to understand that how I behave is as important as who I am! That's what being an expression of God's Love is all about!

Dear God,
May I always have loving and
positive people surrounding me
at all times.

Positive Self-Talk

"I have another question Bob," I said, bending down to tie my shoe.

"Well, then, swing away!" Bob gestures a golf swing with his arms.

"I feel like I'm sabotaging myself with my own negative thoughts. Sometimes I look in the mirror and pick out the flaws I see in my face or my body, and think about all the things I wish I could change about myself. Or, I'm afraid to take on certain projects at work because I'm sure I'll fail miserably and let everyone down, when in-fact, I know I'm the best person for the task. Does that sound crazy, Bob?"

"Not at all, Gena, I completely understand what you are saying," he said with empathy. "Most of us are in a state of constant mental chatter. We talk to ourselves all day long and, unfortunately, this self-talk is frequently negative. Often it is tainted with feelings of guilt about our past or anxiety about our future. This negativity can destroy any seed of hope that we may otherwise have in striving for our dreams." He walked toward the green.

"Take the game of golf, for example," he said. "The mind is the most fearsome opponent that a golfer confronts. So mastering the game of mental golf is essential to our practice." Bob started as we entered the golf course. The day was fine, dry, with a crystalline blue sky.

He cleared his throat and continued. "The mind can be a golfer's best friend, helping to develop the mechanics of a smooth, reliable swing, or its worst foe, thus producing anxiety and tension, which tightens your muscles and destroys your concentration."

I picked up my five iron. It was light, but I gave it a test swing. I had grown accustomed to listening to Bob's long lessons, and I was more than grateful. So I simply nodded, followed along, and listened.

"With that said, the mind is the enemy, and the only way to overcome its powers of self-sabotage is through applying the principles of positive self-talk that yield benefits off the course as well as on. As you've been learning, the two types of energies we possess are negative and positive energy," he said.

"I remember." I volunteered. Bob nodded approvingly.

"As I've said, positive energy makes us feel happy, energized, full of life, inspired, motivated, and healthy; while negative energy makes us feel tired, unhappy, sad, depressed, and angry. If we carry around too much negative energy, this will ultimately create disease in our body." He pulled out his own iron and gave a few practice swings into the air.

"I know what you are saying." I filled the sudden silence. It was my time to talk now. This was how it worked: lesson and response. "I've seen people get really sick after being sad and depressed for a long period of time."

"That's a great observation, Gena. That's exactly how it works. If your mind produces thoughts of stress, anxiety, and insecurity, making you believe that you are not quite good enough the way you are, that something is wrong with you, or that things over which you have no control won't work out, this mental disturbance has a very real impact on your physical health," Bob pointed out.

"I've seen my friends get sick like that from work or home life." I said glumly. "I hated seeing them like that."

"Unfortunately, many people live enslaved by their minds, thoughts, beliefs, mental patterns, and emotions." He turned with a smile on his face. "The good news is that with a little self-awareness and effort, you can begin to free yourself from the negativity of your mind."

"What do you recommend?" I asked as Bob leaned down and placed the ball on the ground.

"Only when we ascend in our consciousness can we fully live in this world as free beings." He drew his club back, hit the ball hard, and watched it sail through the cloudless sky like poetry. "In other words," he turned to me, continuing, "only when we unplug from the *drama* of our negative thinking can we truly be free to live in a state of *peace*."

"Is it just as simple as unplugging from the drama?" I asked.

He smiled knowingly and said, "Before you can break free from negative thoughts, ideas, and beliefs about yourself, your body, and your life, you must first become *aware* of the thoughts that you think on a regular basis."

He handed me a ball. I placed the dimpled white sphere on the grass and stepped back. The hole was almost out of sight, nearly impossible. But then I realized I was being negative.

> ***"Experiencing negative thoughts and feelings from time to time is very normal and serves an important purpose,"*** he said as if he knew.

"For example, feelings of anger, guilt, bitterness and hopelessness are all part of your intuitional guidance system. Negative thoughts and emotions let us know that something in our lives is out of balance."

I nodded, and in the silence I took up my iron and swung as directly as I could. The ball spun through the air. I raised my hand against the sun and watched it travel before it landed nearer to the hole than I expected.

"Yes!" I said, pleased with myself.

"Weren't sure you could do it, huh?" he said, smiling. "As you see, these emotions can provoke us to *ACTION*, help us make decisions and *alert* us to emotional needs that are not being met."

"I love our lessons Bob," I said happily. "Please, do go on," I encouraged him.

"Alright then; if you insist," he said with a grin. He loved nothing more than sharing his knowledge. "So many people cut themselves off from their true essence by dishonoring their emotions and ignoring the signals their bodies send them about the true state of their health, happiness and well-being."

He passed me another ball. I stared at him, puzzled. I already took my shot.

"It's amazing what the mind can think about during the couple seconds of a golf swing, and if you are like most people, those thoughts will often be negative, full of anxiety, or ambivalent about what might happen after you make contact with the ball. In order to master your golf swing, you have to silence your inner critic and practice saying positive things to yourself on a daily basis."

"So, you want me to retake the shot, but be more positive?" I asked. He didn't reply directly. Instead, he smiled widely.

I placed the ball down, stood confidently, and before a single negative thought could enter my mind, I struck the ball. Again, I watched it arc through the air to the hole. It didn't go in, but it was closer! I jumped into the air with joy.

"You see? You have to keep feeding your mind with good thoughts. Self-doubt is an overwhelming obstacle in the game of golf when the negative voice in your head screams so loudly that you end up believing that the messages are actually true," Bob said, beaming.

"It worked." I smiled.

"From now on I just want you to start paying attention to any negative thoughts or doubts that creep into your mind as you move about your day or while practicing your golf swing. The moment you notice a negative thought coming into your mind, replace that thought immediately with a positive one. In doing this you will begin to reprogram your subconscious mind," he said with a big smile.

"What is the subconscious mind?" I asked.

"Your subconscious mind is like one big giant computer. Its function is to store and retrieve the data that you put into it. All of your ways of thinking and acting are stored in your subconscious mind," he explained.

"Oh, I see," I acknowledged.

"Your subconscious mind either grows flowers - good thoughts, or weeds - bad thoughts, depending upon what you feed it," Bob clarified.

"I definitely don't want to grow weeds in my mind," I laughed. "I see why it's important to feed my mind with positive thoughts."

"Exactly. A human mind is like a farmer's land and reminds me of a little parable."

Bob recited the following:

*Suppose a farmer has some land,
and it's good, fertile land.
The land gives the farmer choice.
He may plant in that land whatever he chooses.
The land is not concerned about this.
It's up to the farmer to make the decision.*

*Let us compare the human mind with the land because the mind, like the land doesn't care what you plant in it.
It will return what you plant, but it doesn't care what you plant.*

*Now, let's say that the farmer has two seeds in his hand —
one seed of corn, the other is nightshade, a deadly poison.*

He digs two little holes in the earth and he plants both seeds — one corn, the other nightshade.

*He covers up the holes, waters, and takes care of the land, and what will happen?
Invariably, the land will return what was planted.*

The human mind is far more fertile, far more incredible, far more mysterious than the land, but it works the same way.

*We can plant success or failure.
We can plant a concrete goal or confusion.
We can plant inspiration or depression.*

We can plant courage or fear.
We can plant love for hard work or love for lethargy.

"That is so powerful." I said somewhat dumbstruck, thinking to myself how much sense this all made even though I had never heard it before.

"George Bernard Shaw said, *'People are always blaming their circumstances for what they are. I don't believe in circumstances. The people who get on in this world are the people who get up and look for the circumstances they want, and if they can't find them, they make them.'*" He knelt down, situated the ball on the ground, and without even so much as a pause, the ball sailed through the air.

"In truth, we become what we think about! Now, it stands to reason that a person who is thinking about a concrete and worthwhile goal is going to reach it, because that's what he's thinking about." We just stood almost motionless. Neither of us moved toward our next shot. I just felt compelled to listen intently as he shared from his heart.

"On the opposite side, the person who has no goal who doesn't know where he's going, and whose thoughts must therefore be thoughts of confusion, anxiety, fear and worry, his life becomes one of frustration, fear, anxiety and worry. And if he thinks about nothing, he becomes nothing."

"How does it work?" I asked.

> **"We 'become' what we think about and what we say to ourselves on a daily basis."**

"So just remember that our human mind is just like a farmer's land," he reminded me.

"That's a great analogy!!" I replied.

"What you probably don't also realize is that every thought you have that the subconscious mind processes has an effect on what is *stored* and then *retained* in your subconscious mind. Not only do you have to pay attention to what you tell yourself on a daily basis, but you also have to pay attention to stuff like watching the news on TV, reading a newspaper, watching a violent TV show or anything else that is negative. All have a role in what goes on into your subconscious mind," he said.

"Oh, my gosh. I didn't know that. I watch scary movies all the time. In fact, I couldn't swim in a pool for years after watching the movie *JAWS*," I remarked.

He laughed, "You are not alone in that one, Gena! Most people don't know this, but if you are aware of this early on, you can take immediate steps to correct it by not allowing all this negative information to enter your subconscious mind."

"I won't from now on," I insisted.

"It's imperative that you focus all your attention on information that is encouraging, uplifting, and that supports your happiness and well-being. As you go through the process of reprogramming your subconscious mind, just remember that it doesn't matter what your emotional state may be. Be patient with yourself in the beginning," he cautioned.

"Patience is a virtue and all that, I guess." I smiled.

"Exactly." He returned my smile. "As you begin to replace your old negative thoughts with new healthy thoughts by feeding your mind with healthy information, you will have to stay diligent in your new practice by monitoring what you read and watch on TV so that you don't accidentally remove what you just replaced. In other words, you don't want to reverse the procedure. It's not hard to do; it just takes some work, time, and determination, while also having faith and believing in yourself," he said.

"I never had a strong belief in myself before I met you, but I am learning so many new things. You are inspiring me to become my highest and very best self!" I replied.

"Great!! That's what I like to hear, Gena," he remarked.

"I even wrote a poem about Love this week. Since it's my highest purpose to be an Instrument of Love, I might as well keep talking about it, right?" I asked.

"I couldn't agree with you more. Let's hear it!" he said.

"Okay. It's called *Love Sustains Me*." I stood still and recalled the words I felt compelled to commit to paper the night before:

>*Love is the only True Source that sustains me.*
>*Love is the gift that heals.*
>*It breathes into me its cadence.*
>*I bask in its radiant light and I feel its warm embrace.*
>*It quenches my thirst and feeds my soul.*

> *I can accept this gift of love without reservation.*
> *It brings creativity to my life and awakens my spirit!*
> *Every part of me is gaining strength in Love's energy.*
> *I can feel Love!*
> *I can hear Love!*
> *I can see Love!*
> *I can smell Love!*
> *I can taste Love!*
> *I will walk today in Love's light.*
> *It lifts me up and propels me forward.*
> *There is nothing more that I need, than Love to sustain me.*

"Wow! That was so beautiful! You really are an instrument of Love, Gena," he said with a smile.

"I really am beginning to feel that way, thanks to you," I replied.

"Did I share with you the Prayer of Saint Francis yet?" he beamed.

"No, I but would love to hear it! As you would say, 'Swing away!!'" We both laughed.

"Touché." He nodded, then recited the prayer in a strong, passionate voice.

> *Lord, make me an instrument of Thy peace;*
> *Where there is hatred, let me sow love;*
> *Where there is injury, pardon;*
> *Where there is doubt, faith;*
> *Where there is despair, hope;*
> *Where there is darkness, light;*
> *And where there is sadness, joy.*

O Divine Master,
Grant that I may not so much seek as to be consoled as to console;
To be understood, as to understand;
To be loved, as to love;
For it is in giving that we receive,
It is in pardoning that we are pardoned,
And it is in dying that we are born to eternal life.
Amen

"Wow!! Now that is some powerful self-talk!" We laughed again, not because it was funny, but because we were both happy in sharing knowledge and thoughts.

"Indeed it is! When Saint Francis wrote this passage, he was feeding his mind with flowers in the same way that you are with your lovely poem," Bob pointed out.

Dearest One,

In this lesson, Bob taught me that one of the most powerful influences on our attitude and personality is what we say to ourselves on a daily basis. It is not actually what happens to you, but how you respond internally to what happens to you that will determine your thoughts, feelings, and actions. By controlling your inner dialogue, or your *self-talk,* you can begin to assert control over every part of your life.

We are shaped and molded by what we *BELIEVE*. All that we become is a product of what we think. We have the ability to change our perception when we change our attitude. If you *believe* that you are strong, then you are strong. If you *believe* that you are healthy, then you are healthy. Your thoughts are a *POWERFUL* force that shape your reality and mold your perception. When we walk and talk in a positive vibration, we will run without boundaries or limitations into the light!

I love this quote by Mohandas Gandhi:

> *"Always aim at complete harmony*
> *of thought and word and deed.*
> *Always aim at purifying your thoughts*
> *and everything will be well."*

Dear God,
My inner being contains a luminous light force that is radiant,
translucent, brilliant and bright.
I will therefore create a beautiful
and balanced life.

Creating Confidence By Visualizing Your Outcomes

"I know it's hard to believe, but I have another question," I said with a silly grin on my face.

"Great!!" Bob said, confidently. "I love your questions, Gena. They keep me on my toes!"

I placed my ball on the tee and struck it through the air before asking my question.

"Bob, I think I sometimes lack confidence in myself. Other people seem so sure of themselves; they know what they want from life, and they go for it. I don't hold that same vision. I hold myself back and allow my fears of failure to keep me from trying. Is there something wrong with me?"

"First off, self-confidence is not necessarily a general characteristic which pervades all aspects of a person's life. Typically, we all have some areas of our lives where we feel quite confident, like in the area of sports and/or athletics, while at the same time we do not feel at all confident in other areas, like personal appearance or social relationships." Bob said with kind compassion.

"Let's apply your question to the game of golf.

"One of the biggest problems facing most golfers is a distinct lack of real belief in their own ability. A lack of belief in oneself creates a mental approach of doubt, which causes a whole variety of different problems for players," he explained.

He was correct; I held myself back all the time. As he placed the ball confidently on the ground and stepped up to tee off, he turned back to me with a smile. "When you apply mental visualization to your game, you will discover a whole range of extra benefits that go far beyond the game of golf into daily life." Bob swung, sending the ball through the air. He barely looked at it, and yet it seemed to go exactly where he wanted it to go.

"Great shot," I complimented, and he smiled wider. He took another ball, but this time gestured for me to take it. "Thanks," I said.

"Mental visualization can be used to help you overcome extreme nervousness or anxiety. It can help boost your confidence, conquer intimidation, and defeat self-criticism. It can dramatically increase your own inner belief. It can even increase your energy, enthusiasm, and motivation." He paused. "Go on, take your shot." As I moved in to position, Bob continued to talk away. He was a big talker, but boy was I glad he was.

"To get the most out of your game, you will have to treat every shot like it's the most important shot of your life."

"OK," I said, swinging back my club, readying for the next shot. I concentrated hard, but before I took my shot, Bob spoke again.

"That means that you will have to visualize every shot you want to hit and make sure that you are 100% sure of what you are going to do before you make contact with the ball. You shouldn't have any doubts of whether or not you can pull off the shot you are about to hit."

"Got it," I said confidently though I wasn't feeling too sure about the whole idea. I let the club rest and stepped out of swinging position. He really had me thinking now, and I couldn't possibly take a shot with all these thoughts and questions running through my head... *OK, I've got to hit the ball over the water...please God, just let the wind come up behind me and carry the ball over that sand trap...is my grip right? Seriously, don't hit it in the water...I only have two more balls left...boy, that's a big bee...I wonder if Bob can hear my stomach growling...I really need to get some new golf shoes...I hope I don't hit a lot of traffic on my drive home...I really don't want to go to work on Monday.*

"What you are explaining to me sounds a lot like our lesson when I was hitting golf balls with my eyes closed, but this time you are just talking a lot more and trying to distract me," I retorted.

He laughed and said, "That's exactly right, Gena! I just can't seem to hit anything past you these days," Bob said, laughing hysterically at my candor and yet another of his silly golf puns.

I couldn't help but laugh with him. Once we regained our composure, Bob began to speak again.

"I can tell you have been paying attention to our lessons and have developed the keen ability to apply what you are learning to future insights. You are going to become a great teacher of truth one day," he said in a complimentary way.

"Me? A teacher?" I replied, doubtful.

"Of course! What else did you think you were up to? This is what you're preparing yourself for!"

"I am?" I still didn't sound convinced.

Bob caught me off guard with the whole teacher comment, but a feeling of excitement stirred within me at the very thought of it. I drifted off into some future time picturing myself in this role. I sensed Bob was 'validating' what I knew deep down was my highest calling and deepest desire. He rattled me with his comment because I felt as though he reached into my soul a saw a part of me that I never shared with anyone before. How could he possibly know this about me?

As I mused, Bob gently brought me back to the present moment and lesson at hand.

He gently cleared his throat so as not to startle me and continued, "As you recall from our previous lesson, we don't learn a golf swing by memorizing the how-to, but rather by creating a picture (a mental visualization) in our *mind's eye* of us making the proper motion. With mental visualization we can teach our body how to make the proper motion to produce consistent, predictable results, even with our eyes closed.

"Another crucial element when you visualize playing a round of golf in your mind's eye is to use all your senses. For example, imagine seeing the greens, the fairways, and surroundings all in their respective colors, and most of all *feel* that amazing joy of victory when you shoot a fabulous round," he said, looking out to the green.

"I definitely think about winning!" I exclaimed. "Not sure I have the skill to match it quite yet."

"Don't ever doubt or limit your ability, Gena. The only trouble we encounter is within our own limited minds," he said emphatically. "Self-doubt has the power to cause extreme disturbance in your life, not only because it makes you feel powerless and out of control, but also because it triggers you to act in ways that are usually counterproductive to what you want to accomplish like winning a golf match."

He saw my thoughtful expression as I concentrated on what he was saying and went on, "Mental visualization is about picturing and experiencing with the full resources of your imagination your desired outcomes accomplished in the present moment. If you do this for every practice session here at the range, you will begin to gradually notice a shift in your confidence levels and your results will steadily improve."

As we packed our equipment into our caddy, Bob said, "The same concept applies to daily life you know. Think about what you want to become and what your highest vision of yourself is."

"Right now?" I asked, a little perplexed.

"Yes, right now. Take a few moments right now to reflect on some personality traits you would like to embody. Obviously, self-confidence will be one of the traits, but consider other traits you'd like to have, like compassion, kindness, integrity, and so on."

"Once you establish a few personality traits you would like to embody, close your eyes and call up a mental image of your current self. Does your current *self* happen to have any of the traits you've just visualized?" he asked.

"Yes, a couple of them, but I'd like them to become stronger, more prevalent," I replied.

"Okay, good!" He seemed really pleased with my participation in this lesson and continued, "Simply imagine that those traits are beginning to become obvious in this mental image of yourself. For example, you might see yourself standing a bit taller, smiling with happiness and purpose, or wearing an expression of peacefulness and confidence on your face," he envisioned.

"Yes, I can see that! It feels good!" I said, getting excited about the possibilities.

"Great! Now just keep adding more and more visual cues to this mental image of yourself until you can see yourself as the person you want to be. It will probably take more than this one session to gain a clear and strong mental image of the *NEW YOU*, but do the very best you can. The more practice, the easier it will become," he assured me.

Bob became more passionate and said, "Now, as you look at this strong, confident person in your mind's eye, begin to switch your focus slightly so that you are *FEELING* and behaving as she does, mimicking her demeanor and posture. Feel yourself growing more confident, self-assured, impassioned about your highest purpose, motivated about your goals, and so on. Really see yourself interacting in your daily life with newfound confidence and enthusiasm! Stay with this inner vision for as long as you can, making it *FEEL* as real as possible," he paused to catch his breath.

"Then, even after you return to your normal activities, be sure to keep calling to mind a mental picture of this new you as often as you can, and make an attempt to feel and act like that person did during this visualization process. Rather than reacting with doubt to situations like you normally would, pause and remember that you are now a confident, self-assured person," he insisted. "The more you shift your focus to express this new version of your highest self, the easier it will become to keep it going and gradually become that person inside and out!"

"This is so encouraging, Bob! Even though I only practiced this for a short amount of time, I can already feel the difference within," I said, exhilarated and tuned-in to who I wanted to be.

"Perfect, that's exactly what I want to hear!" he exclaimed. "This mental visualization exercise will provide the inspiration and the motivation from which to draw by taking God The Living Spirit into your body and mind. When you believe in your dreams and really feel them from your soul, you create space and opportunities for your dreams to be realized. You will shed your fear of the impossible, and open your heart, mind, and spirit to the possible! As Winston Churchill said, '*Never, never, never give up!*'" He finished putting the clubs away, and rubbed his hands together.

"Let's go to the clubhouse and get a drink. I'll tell you a story on the way about two cockroaches that lived in a house," he said as he walked toward me.

"Where do you come up with all these stories?" I asked.

"I've been around a really long time!" He chuckled before continuing with his story:

> *There once lived two cockroaches that lived in a house. Both cockroaches were young and full of energy. Each day, they would run, jump, and chase each other while playing. Though they were equally strong, there was a difference. One cockroach was optimistic and always lived in hope, while the other was pessimistic and lived in despair.*
>
> *One day, while playing, both cockroaches fell into a pot of milk. They swam around and tried to hop out, but, as there was no solid support under their feet, it was not possible for the cockroaches to hop out and escape from the pot.*
>
> *After some struggle, the pessimistic cockroach said to itself, 'It is impossible to hop out. No doubt, I have strength but I can't swim very long. I am already tired.'*

Thinking thus, the cockroach did become tired soon and could not swim any longer. It gave up its struggle and went down to the bottom of the pot. Finally, it drowned.

On the other hand, the optimistic cockroach kept on struggling, saying to itself, "No doubt, it seems difficult, but who knows? If I try a little longer, something good might happen. It is a question of only a few minutes more, and then I will be out of here."

The second cockroach went on swimming. His constant leg movements churned the milk and turned it into a huge heap of butter. Soon the cockroach was able to climb up the heap of butter and hopped out of the pot.

"Another great story," I applauded as we walked to the clubhouse. Bob was inexhaustible.

"Positive thinking had saved the life of the cockroach, and nothing is impossible as long as you don't give up! When you visualize, you need to have a strong desire, motivation from within, and the commitment to do whatever is necessary to achieve your goal," he insisted.

"I will do my very best to make mental visualization part of my daily routine. My mom always visualizes planting her garden before the spring season arrives. Every night before she goes to bed, she visualizes the way she wants her garden to look each year. She tends to the garden in her mind before planting seeds or performing any of the physical work," I said.

"So, you are already familiar with mental visualization?" Bob asked excitedly.

"I never understood why she did this, but she must have understood the principle of mental visualization," I explained.

"I sense that your mother is a very smart woman, and she has prepared you well to be an instrument of Love!" Bob replied.

"Yes, she truly is and she has. I can see this now. She always tells me to follow my heart's desire." I smiled at the thought of my mother. "She said I have to see my heart's desire in my mind first and then feel it in my Heart. '*When my heart and mind are united,*' she said, '*you will never give up.*' You will have the strength inside you to do whatever it takes to accomplish your goal. I can see how all my experiences have been preparing me to live in the Light of my highest purpose."

"Thank you, Bob, for helping me to realize what I couldn't see until now."

Dearest One,

When Bob told me that I was going to be a great teacher someday, I had serious doubt because I didn't feel *worthy* enough to be a teacher. I certainly wasn't feeling confident in my own abilities at that time in my life.

Ever since I can remember, I've always wanted to help people see the joy and beauty *within* themselves and free themselves of fear and negativity. What he said excited me because he gave me a sense of hope, vision, and belief in myself that I would one day be able to help people in the same way that he helped me.

Bob clearly showed me that confidence is a state of mind. Confidence comes from the belief in our own ability, and must keep reinforcing that belief through our conscious thoughts and our daily actions.

> **To feel confident we have to stop thinking about what we 'CAN'T' do and start focusing on what we 'CAN' do and take the necessary steps to achieve that.**

For example, how we choose to speak to ourselves and how we impress images upon the subconscious mind all have a direct connection to our outward experience.

It is through our *efforts* to recreate our self-image that we will bring forth the outcomes we desire. For instance, when we visualize ourselves stepping into our highest power, we begin to *feel* the possibility of achieving that from within. When this happens, we catch a glimpse of our desired future and are motivated and prepared to pursue our highest good in our daily conduct and actions. The art of visualization is a powerful *tool* for achieving positive behavioral change and creating the life we desire!

I love this quote by Robert Collier:

> *"Visualize this thing that you want; see it, feel it, believe in it. Make your mental blue print, and begin to build."*

Self-Love and Acceptance

We sat down in the clubhouse with our drinks and Bob continued his lesson.

"As I was saying, it's important to develop a certain level of confidence in the game of golf by visualizing your outcomes. You must have confidence in yourself and belief in your ability to complete certain tasks in order to bring your best game forward."

"That's easier said than done." I smiled, sipping my iced tea.

"True." He laughed. "But we have to believe in our own abilities to go out there and perform at our very best! We also have to have confidence in ourselves in our daily life, which is simply having an appropriate love of self."

"I've never been very good at giving myself much credit for the things I do," I said honestly. He nodded in understanding.

"Gena, self-love is not a selfish kind of love like you might think. Self-love is an act of being loving and happy with who you are right now. For example, when you love who you are right now, you believe that you are enough in and of yourself because you are the embodiment of God.

"When you love who you are right now, you never put yourself down or feel inadequate or unworthy. You trust that God The Living Spirit is always on your side and is working on your behalf according to the divine plan. This is the meaning of faith.

"When you love who you are right now, you honor your own needs without having to seek outside approval and are able to cultivate the peace of inner silence. You come to terms with your entire self, both your good and bad aspects—you are in balance.

"When you love who you are right now you feel grateful for every part of your soul's journey," he said.

"What you just said is so very beautiful. I've never looked at myself in this way before. I suppose I haven't been honoring the spirit within me because I have always put so much emphasis on the way other people see me."

"Most people do." Bob nodded.

"I guess I've always rated my value according to the approval that I receive from others. For a long time I believed my body, for example, wasn't good enough, and I allowed my desire to have a perfect body take over my life. It didn't matter that I was strong; it didn't matter that I was flexible, or that I was athletic. To me it was all about how I looked on the outside," I said.

"I hear and understand what you are saying, Gena. The truth is that you cannot control what other people think of you or how they view you. People have their own agenda; they come with their own baggage of self-doubt and insecurities. When we look to the approval of others, we live unhappy and limited lives, denying ourselves happiness and failing to do the things we really want to do because we are too worried about what other people will *think*."

"Very true," I agreed. I leaned back in my chair and took in the surroundings of the club bar. I'd never been inside before; it was a beautiful mix of mahogany furnishings and red leather seats. I turned back to Bob to encourage him to continue.

"You know Gena, God is more concerned about our hearts than our appearance. You are made to be the unique person you are. There is no one else on earth who looks or behaves exactly like you. No one else has your same personality or physical qualities. This brings me to a story that I want to share with you about the cracked pot whose unique flaws served a valuable purpose."

"Another story?" I half teased. "I do love your stories, Bob."

"I'm glad you do." He laughed. "This is an appropriate one for our discussion I promise. You see, Gena, we're all cracked pots in some way. Our cracks aren't flaws because they allow the light to shine through us." He began his story:

> *A water bearer had two large pots; each hung on the ends of a pole which he carried across his neck.*
>
> *One of the pots had a crack in it, while the other pot was perfect and always delivered a full portion of water.*

At the end of the long walk from the stream to the house, the cracked pot arrived only half full.

For a full two years this went on daily, with the bearer delivering only one and a half pots full of water to his house.

Of course, the perfect pot was proud of its accomplishments, perfect for which it was made.

But the poor cracked pot was ashamed of its own imperfection and miserable that it was able to accomplish only half of what it had been made to do.

After two years of what it perceived to be a bitter failure, it spoke to the water bearer one day by the stream.

"I am ashamed of myself, and I want to apologize to you. I have been able to deliver only half my load because this crack in my side causes water to leak out all the way back to your house. Because of my flaws, you have to do all of this work, and you don't get full value from your efforts," the pot said.

The bearer said to the pot, "Did you notice that there were flowers only on your side of the path, but not on the other pot's side?

"That's because I have always known about your flaw, and I planted flower seeds on your side of the path, and every day while we walk back, you've watered them. For

two years I have been able to pick these beautiful flowers to decorate the table. Without you being just the way you are, there would not be this beauty to grace the house.'"

Dearest One,

Bob's beautiful lesson taught me that self-love and acceptance don't come from changing myself into something *better* because I am already beautiful and perfect just the way I am. When God made me, He made me exactly the way he planned me to be. When he designed me, even before I was born, he planned my size, the color of my eyes, the color of my skin, and every beautiful and wonderful thing about me.

The ability to love one's self is the core and foundation of our ability to love others and to love God. When you practice self-love, you send a message to the Universe that you are *worthy*. In fact you are a divine being! Not to love yourself is to deny your own spirit.

> **When we truly love ourselves,**
> **we take pride in who we are**
> **and what we have to offer.**
> **We can't see or appreciate**
> **the beauty in others**
> **if we can't see or even**
> **appreciate the beauty within ourselves.**

Bob illuminated the beautiful truth that God—The Infinite Intelligence–doesn't make anything flawed or imperfect.

> **I am wonderfully and beautifully made**
> **and the light of God within me IS the**
> **beauty that shines through me!**

I don't need to conform to somebody else's standard of success or beauty because I am already successful and beautiful in the eyes of God, my Creator! I could feel the energy of all the new and beautiful possibilities for my life with this new insight.

Dear God,
I believe that every part of me is beautiful and therefore my energy releases a positive light into the world!

Be True, Be You

"I loved that story of the cracked pot, Bob, because I sometimes feel different from other people. However, I feel that if I reveal my true self that it will create friction with other people, and they won't like or accept me for who I am. Sometimes I feel completely alone in this world. Does this make any sense?" I asked.

"Gena, it does make sense to me. However, I believe it's better for your soul to do what comes naturally and not to feel like you have to change or compromise yourself in order to get by in this world. Even when being true to yourself creates some friction, it is worth it in exchange for being able to live day-to-day knowing that you're staying true to your values.

"Occasionally, you will run into people who are walking embodiments of the average, mainstream person whose every whim just happens to fall into line with what society prefers. However, there are many people who have a myriad of traits that are out of sync with whatever the social ideal is, and they stay true to themselves anyway.

"If you feel that you are different from the norm, you do not have to conform just to make others around you happy or comfortable. Whatever you're like, and whatever you're into, you can find a group of like-minded people to fall in with. People naturally sort themselves into groups based on similarities. Obviously, you're going to feel happier, more accepted, and less constrained around people you have something in common with.

"Golf is a great way to meet like-minded people who have similar interests, but even in this situation people will sometimes hide their true nature. Does that make sense?" Bob got up to stretch.

We finished our drinks and headed back to play another nine holes.

"There is a saying that you cannot hide your true personality in golf." Bob handed me a club. "I think this is undoubtedly true." He smiled. "Golf may not be as loud and as fast as some other sports are, but you sure get to know all kinds of people and their temperaments playing a round."

"Well, I'm thoroughly enjoying getting to know you." I said.

"Likewise," Bob smiled again before setting the ball down. "I played once with a golfer by the name of John, who was one of the most pleasant people I've ever met *off* the course. However, put a club in his hand for 18 holes, and he morphed into the Dark Avenger, seething and cursing over every missed shot."

"Oh, that's not good." I said.

"John started off the round with a smile, a handshake, and some friendly banter. By around the fourth hole and several flubbed shots, he cursed and berated himself for playing the game. At the back nine, he tossed his clubs that went like a whirlybird through the air and sometimes ended up farther down the fairway than his shot."

"Wow, hope I don't have to play anyone like him anytime soon!"

"The truth is, Gena, many of us spend our lives wearing different masks or facades. The more of these masks we wear, the deeper we hide our true selves. I'd recommend you really try not doing something or pretending to be someone else for the sake of gaining acceptance. That's one of the reasons I told you the cracked pot story earlier."

"Another great story to add to the collection," I smiled.

"Well, I hope you do share them." He nodded. "All I want is for you to have the courage to accept yourself as you really are, not as someone else thinks you should be because sooner or later your true nature will be exposed anyway. When you do things that are not genuine or reflect the real you, you will not be happy with yourself, and you'll end up confused because you won't know who to please or how."

"That's true enough," I said as Bob took his shot. It went wide of the hole, but he didn't seem unhappy, I wondered if this was also meant to be a lesson. I wouldn't judge, and he wouldn't care!

"Self-respect comes from being true to who you really are and from acting in accordance with your fundamental nature. When you respect yourself, others will respect you in return."

"It's a great idea, but again, easier said than done."

"Again, yes. Being true to yourself takes strength and courage. It requires you to be introspective, sincere, honest, open-minded, and fair. It doesn't mean that you are inconsiderate or disrespectful of others. It means that you will not let others define you or make decisions for you that you should make for yourself. Not everyone is going to like you, and that's *OK*!

"Well, Gena, I'll admit I have loved playing golf with you, and it seems to get better each time. Not just your golf game, mind you, but your willingness to listen to all my ramblings and pretend it's fascinating and useful information. You have been good for my soul, and I feel that you will take these lessons and do great things with them. Try to put some of these ideas to practice this week, and I'll see you next time."

On the drive home I thought about my discussion with Bob about being true to myself and how it takes strength and courage. As I pondered our conversation, I distinctly recalled being nine years old and my dad taking me to see the movie *Jonathan Livingston Seagull*. I still vividly remember the movie and how inspired I was by it.

The movie tells the story of an unusual seagull named Jonathan Livingston Seagull. This very special seagull symbolizes unlimited freedom. Jonathan the seagull is frustrated with the material world and the idea of conforming to the mundane existence of seagull life, of simply scurrying around for food, trying to survive, living unconsciously, and reacting to the environment of fighting, struggling, and competing.

But Jonathan is different.

His heart is filled with passion for flights of all kinds, and he looks for ways to fly always upward towards his Higher Self. Often flying is symbolic of higher learning.

His lack of conformity and his passion for higher knowledge eventually lead to conflict with his flock, and he is cast out from their society. They reject him because they didn't understand him. In fact they feared him.

As a result, Jonathan is ostracized. Along his journey he meets up with several master teachers who eventually teach him the highest of life's lessons.

In the end, Jonathan returns back to his flock demonstrating his own act of surrender and forgiveness toward his flock for banishing him. Jonathan understands that they are just living *unconsciously* and don't know any better.

He goes back and shares his newly discovered wisdom with anyone in the flock who will listen, despite the conflict he knows he will face.

Jonathan becomes a master teacher with the understanding that *Love* is the answer and the ability to *forgive* is freedom.

He discovers that to become a teacher is his greatest gift and offering.

I loved Jonathan's ability to soar above the earth and the ocean, feeling the wind and the sun and the freedom of moving without restriction. He was being true to himself and he was in love with life!

At the end of the movie my father asked me if I understood the message of the seagull.

I said, "The message of the seagull is to Love."

After seeing that movie I wanted a Jonathan Livingston Seagull lunchbox more than anything else in the world. At that time, super hero lunch boxes like Wonder Woman, Batman and the Incredible Hulk were the *thing* to have, but Jonathan Livingston Seagull was *my* superhero.

I was so excited to bring my new lunchbox to school and show it off to all my friends. I was so proud of it. When I took my lunch box to school some of the kids made fun of it. They said that my lunch box was stupid and that the bird was dumb.

One boy actually grabbed it out of my hands and threw it on the ground.

Later that evening I was crying and my dad asked me what happened. I told him about the mean boy at school, and he asked me what I loved most about Jonathan.

I answered, "What I most love about Jonathan is that he loves to fly and that he is brave."

My dad replied, "Gena, don't ever be ashamed to stand up for the things that you love or believe in. As long as you are true to yourself, you will never have reason to be afraid."

Bob's lesson really hit home today.

Dear God,
I will find my rainbow through time.
I will follow its colors for they light my path.
I will trust my judgment for it is my guide.
I won't turn back when I'm just getting started -
the time is now to take a risk.
When I find my rainbow, I won't be too tired to climb it.
I've come too far.

Dearest One,

In this lesson, Bob taught me that being true to myself is about being genuine and real. Being true also allows us to connect on a deeper and more intimate level with others because it requires us to be transparent and vulnerable. We must drop the false pretenses and stop being something or someone else. Liberation comes when we finally realize that we don't need to be perfect and composed for people to love us.

Being true to yourself begins when you set the intention to be genuine. When you live with this kind of self-awareness, decisions are easier because you are free to choose things that move you closer to your highest values. When you are able to stand in the presence of your imperfections and accept your humanity, you are more likely to embrace your unique talents, gifts, and abilities with courage, grace and dignity. And others will be drawn to your commitment to be uniquely and truly YOU!

I love this quote by William Shakespeare:

"*This above all; to thine own self be true.*"

Be Grateful

I woke up this morning feeling a little sad and indifferent. I couldn't quite understand why I was feeling this way, especially since Saturday is my favorite day of the week to spend with Bob. I pulled out my poem journal to write down my thoughts, and I noticed a passage that I wrote several years ago.

Dear God,
Why do I find conflict in the simplest things, taking precious moments for granted? I'm searching and reaching for a destination, but when will I know when I've arrived? Will it be good enough?
As I push and pull myself toward my destination, reaching for the goal, I'm taking for granted the ride and scenery as it slowly passes me by.
The destination is all around me and I'm touching it every day.
I just have to learn how to feel it.

When I arrived at the course Bob greeted me with his usual friendly smile, which immediately warmed my heart and lifted my mood, but he somehow sensed that I was feeling a little down.

"I'm sensing that your thoughts are a little heavy today, Gena," Bob said, in a concerned yet compassionate tone. "Let's start walking to the first tee. This will raise your energy levels and get your blood flowing from your long drive. You can fill me in on the way."

We walked briskly to the first tee off, and I immediately started in with my questioning.

"Bob, sometimes I feel completely satisfied with my life, and other times I feel like nothing's quite right. I often have this nagging feeling that I'm missing out on something. How do I get more consistent on feeling good about my life?"

"Gena, being grateful, counting your blessings, noticing simple pleasures, and acknowledging everything that you receive will help shift the way you look at life in general. Learning to live your life as if everything were a miracle, and being aware on a continual basis of how much you've been given turns your life from mundane to miraculous! Being grateful shifts your focus from what your life lacks to the abundance that is already present." Bob smiled and continued.

"Golf is a great sport for developing a state of gratitude.

"Despite the enjoyment a great golf shot will bring you, golf is a game of misses, too, and it always will be." Bob looked back at his wide shot and shrugged. He brushed it off as easily as if it hadn't happened.

"My shot." I stepped up to the tee.

"This also applies to our lives," he said behind me, "so I encourage you to feel grateful for everything that happens to you, both the good experiences and the bad experiences alike. No matter what's going on in your outside experience, no matter what cards life is dealing you, no matter what emotional place you are at right now, there is always a way to apply a little gratitude," he said. I nodded but I didn't turn around. Instead I took my shot. It was neither here nor there; I couldn't place it as good or bad, so I thought that was okay.

"Sincere gratitude is an act of Love," Bob continued. He pulled out a different club and passed it to me.

"But why would I want to be grateful for all the sadness and disappointments in my life?" I asked.

"Because it's easy to feel grateful about the positive things in life, but it's not as easy to feel grateful about all the disappointments that you encounter."

"Boy, you can sure say that again!"

"The practice of being thankful for 'everything' is like strengthening a muscle. As you make the conscious effort each day to incorporate gratitude as a way of *being,* your appreciation for *all* things will grow and strengthen over time." Bob looked over at my ball, wildly far from the hole by his standards, but he didn't look concerned. He passed me another ball, and with the new club I took the shot again.

"When your attention is focused on your mistakes, failures, injustices, and disappointments, then you are focusing on lack and limitation, which will prevent you from noticing all the good stuff that is happening around you." We looked at my shot again, still wide.

"Why can't I get it near?" I asked.

"Perhaps because you are focusing too much on the idea that you haven't gotten it near enough, rather than thinking positively that you *can* make the shot, or seeing what is great about that shot."

"Actually that makes sense to me!" I exclaimed, surprised at this realization.

"Whenever you focus your attention on lacking something, you are separating yourself from all the abundant blessings of God. I'll tell you a little story to illustrate what living gratitude might look like, as I know you love my stories." He smiled my way and began:

> *Two men were walking along one summer day. Soon it became too hot to go any farther, and seeing a large plane tree nearby, they threw themselves on the ground to rest in its shade. Gazing up into the branches, one man said to the other, "What a useless tree this is. It does not have fruit or nuts that we can eat and we cannot even use its wood for anything."*
>
> *"Don't be so ungrateful," rustled the tree in reply. "I am being extremely useful to you at this very moment, shielding you from the hot sun. And you call me a good-for-nothing!"*

He finished, and continued with the lesson.

"Always count your blessings, be thankful for what you do have, and you will be rewarded with more of the good things. Think back on some of the unpleasant experiences in your life. Some of these experiences may have led you to new growth or to even better things, places, and people than you may have ever imagined were possible."

"I try to count my blessings." I sounded a little defensive, standing there with my arms crossed over my chest.

"Being able to shift gears and see the opportunities in crisis can make bad times easier to deal with. Even small amounts of positive emotions, if you focus on them regularly, can help you develop your skills and strategies for coping with adversity."

"What do you advise doing?"

"Each morning, start to spend a few minutes focusing on everything in your life that you can be grateful for. Most importantly, practice every day being grateful for what you already have. Any time you have a problem, or you find yourself struggling with something, just calm down and ask God 'within' you for some help and guidance. When you do this, the indwelling Spirit will create even more items of abundance for you to truly feel good about."

"It sounds like something I could put into practice and from what you are saying it could yield some pretty amazing results," I said.

"Don't worry about clearing out all of your lack of gratitude or any negativity overnight either. This is a gradual process, and you must sincerely feel gratitude taking over your being. You can't deny or run away from your negative emotions, or life will throw you something equally as testing until you completely change your perspective from drudgery, disappointment, and frustration to one of joy, gratitude, and abundance." He looked at me, checking to see if what he was saying was too much.

I was keenly interested in everything Bob had to say, as I tilted my head to one side.

Satisfied that I absorbed his words, he said, "In changing your old habitual responses, be patient and forgiving of yourself, and begin with baby steps. For example, if you have lost a loved one in death, allow yourself to appreciate the time spent together and the joy and growth you had. Realize that all relationships are eternal and you will always be connected in some form.

"You can even be grateful for the sadness you feel for it shows that you are compassionate, open, tender-hearted and loving. An open heart naturally attracts abundance, love, and joy. Slowly begin to let go of having all your needs met at all times.

"Instead, redirect your attention to other possibilities that can bring you abundance. Open yourself up to something better by becoming a more grateful and loving person.

"When you unplug from the internal struggle, you avoid a lot of stress and unhappiness.

"Applying gratitude everywhere in your life will be uncomfortable in the beginning, but it will become second nature for it is the essence of your highest self."

I paused to absorb what Bob was saying. "Everything that you are saying makes so much sense to me, Bob. When things are tough, or when I'm going through a rough patch, it's easy for me to get caught up in all of the things that seem wrong. I sometimes have a tendency to dwell on the negative and quickly find myself falling into a negative frame of mind. When this happens my energy and productivity levels drop. I become less motivated to accomplish anything and fall into a state of indifference."

"This is a great observation, Gena. Every negative thought we have drains our energy and diminishes our valuable supply of life energy. You need all your energy to discover, fully embrace and live your passion, and realize your divine purpose. How can you do that when you are focused on what isn't working, or on what you don't like or don't want?"

"I definitely see what you mean. So, is it wrong of me to want something more, better, or different, instead of fully rejoicing in what I already have? I sometimes yearn for other possibilities beyond what I already have," I said.

"When your ego is dissatisfied or discontent in what you already have, then you most likely are experiencing a certain level of ungratefulness. But if you want something more, better, or different for the glory of God or for the benefit of helping others, this feeling may be a sign of your devotion or of your love for something bigger that wants to be expressed through you."

"I never thought of it this way before. This makes me feel so much better and gives me hope, encouragement, and a whole new perspective! I will practice saying *thank you* for both my happy times and my challenging times. I will count my blessings every day and honor God for all that is. I will express my appreciation to everything and everyone I encounter in the spirit of love."

"That's wonderful, Gena! Gratitude is also an interactive spiral between a giver and a receiver. It recognizes that a gift has been given. It recognizes a favor done by someone for us. Gratitude is also a response to that gift. We thank the giver with an expression of appreciation. A gesture of gratitude completes the circle and lets the loving act flow from the giver to receiver and then back to the giver again.

Such an exchange opens us up to another exchange. The gesture of thanks moves both the giver and receiver to another level. In realizing that God showers us with gifts, we also recognize our oneness (unity) with God. Having received a blessing and a gift, we acknowledge his goodness, his love for us, and his grace by responding with gratitude. The circle is complete, and it allows us to open yet a deeper part of our life and our hearts."

He got that mischievous look on his face. "This brings me to the story of *The Peach Tree and the Earth Worm*. It's about the power of giving and receiving and balancing the good with the not so good."

Once upon a time a farmer planted a peach tree in fertile soil.

Underneath the peach tree there lived a big earthworm, called a night crawler.

It went through the soil by digging tunnels, and then using those tunnels to travel.

It came up, usually at night and sometimes on wet rainy days, to eat the rotting leaves laying on top of the ground.

It helped recycle the leaves by eating them and then turning them into castings to fertilize the soil.

It went deep into the ground if the weather above was too hot or too cold.

Now the peach tree grew fast.

Every Spring, it woke up.

It had to bloom, grow leaves and bigger branches, and finally when it was old enough have fruit by Summer, else the farmer might chop it down.

Then in the Fall when it got colder, its leaves would change color and fall onto the ground.

It was dormant all Winter long.

As the peach tree grew, it found out how difficult it was to grow its roots directly into the hard dirt.

It looked for an easier way.

So it began to grow its roots into the tunnels the night crawler had made.

As the tree grew, its roots also grew, and soon the night crawler's tunnels were plugged shut.

The night crawler could not come up for food. So, in order to stay alive and keep from starving, it had to dig more tunnels.

It did not like to do this because night crawlers are sort of lazy.

And the peach tree didn't like shedding its leaves each Fall just before the cold winter.

But do you know what?

They were both helping each other, and by doing this, they were actually helping themselves.

The peach tree had to shed its leaves which the earthworm ate and the earthworm's castings fed the peach tree.

And the earthworm had to dig more tunnels which allowed the peach tree to grow bigger so that in the Fall there were plenty of good leaves (and maybe a peach or two that the farmer missed) for the earthworm to eat.

And they all lived happily ever after.

Dearest One,

When you are in a sincere state of gratitude, your energy is one of acceptance, balance and harmony. Gratitude forms once you realize what you have been given, who you *ARE,* and from whom all blessings flow.

We can never say *Thank You* enough to God and Mother Earth for providing us with the miracle of life and the blessings of sustainability. When giving thanks becomes an integral part of your life, you will find that your attitude toward life will *CHANGE*. You will become a more positive, gracious, loving, and humble person.

I really feel as though Bob's life changing golf lessons were meant to prepare me for my future "now self."

I knew right away when I met Bob that I was experiencing something phenomenal and out of the ordinary, but I was still naive in my understanding at that time. I still had much of life to live, and I certainly made many mistakes along the way. Bob showed me in his dramatic telling of the *Pencil* story how I became a better person through some of my most painful sharpenings.

It's been said that hindsight is 20/20. I see now how everything is connected, leading me to exactly where I am today. As Bob would say, "*No matter what the situation you find yourself in, you must continue to live your highest purpose.*"

CHAPTER 13

Experience Nature

The crisp morning air prompted me to grab a windbreaker from my closet before heading out the door. I ran late and felt anxiety pulsing through my body because I couldn't find my things for today's lesson with Bob and frantically searched my apartment. All week long, the stress and pressure of work and school built up within until I felt completely overwhelmed. School finals and work deadlines occupied my thoughts, and I had no idea how to find a sense of peace and balance in my current state of unrest and chaos. I wondered if Bob could give me some insight that would help me calm down.

On the drive to Napa, the Sutter Butte Mountains rose in the distance, bringing back the memory of a backpacking trip with my father. On one particular hiking excursion, Dad climbed a mountain ridge in order to get a panoramic view of the lake below. When we finally reached the summit, we saw the lake and the mountain valley stretching for miles. It was beautiful, peaceful, and serene. On the ridge, the cool breeze caressed my face and the wind rustled the trees.

The view was breathtaking! Reaching the summit after such an arduous hike rewarded us with the glorious scene below and moved me close to tears. Dad and I stood in silence absorbing the moment. I felt peace. The beauty of the landscape completely embraced and consumed me. The sense of oneness with the world, my father, and my Creator etched itself deep within my soul.

After a few minutes of silence, Dad said something to me that I didn't fully understand at the time, but I remember it like it was yesterday. He said, "Gena, whenever you are feeling anxious or overwhelmed, always remember this moment and come back to it in your *mind*. This will be your place of solace where you can slow down your thoughts and reconnect with the heart of God."

When I arrived at the golf range, my thoughts had settled, but I still wanted to ask Bob how to maintain a sense of calm in the midst of my busy lifestyle. Bob approached me with his usual grin and welcoming demeanor.

I wanted his advice, so I said, "Bob, I've been feeling completely overwhelmed lately. How do I become more peaceful and happy in the midst of a full and demanding schedule?" I am so focused on my new career and moving up in the company. Plus, I am taking night classes in writing, psychology, philosophy, and art. Finding time to relax seems impossible. I'm up at 5 am, hit the ground running, work all day and barely have time to eat dinner."

"Gena, many of us are shut in our homes, offices, cars, or trains most of the time, and rarely do we get the chance to go outside in the fresh air. You can really learn to create a sense of peace and balance in your life by taking the time to go outside and really observe nature. Take a deep breath of the fresh air, and enjoy the serenity of water and greenery out here on the course. Really feel the sensations of water, wind, and earth against your skin." Bob paused, turned his face toward the sun, and breathed deeply. With a satisfying sigh, he said, "If you don't take time for personal reflection and contemplation, you will lose touch with your spirit and innermost purpose."

"You're right, Bob. It certainly feels good to be getting out here in the open air." I took a deep breath. "That's one of the things I love most about golf. I always get this incredible feeling being out in wide open spaces and standing firmly on the beautifully kept grounds. It conjures up all kinds of fond memories, especially those hiking trips with my dad. Something about it always makes me feel like everything is right with the world. Does that make any sense to you, Bob?" I asked.

"It sure does, Gena, whether you spend half an hour at the driving range, play a few holes or a full game, golf will always take you outside into some of the country's most beautiful green spaces. Being outside surrounded by nature is good for your spirit and emotional well-being. I have always used the quietness of the golf course to center myself and focus on the simpler things in life. The game of golf allows me to be immersed in the beauty and tranquility of nature and always brings out the best in me," he replied.

Standing like a professor in front of a blackboard, scratching his chin, Bob said in his best scientific-like voice, "It's been scientifically proven that through the oxygen boost from fresh air produces natural feel-good chemicals in your body. Meanwhile, the green surroundings have shown calm one down, reduce blood pressure and stress hormones, and promote a feeling of just being away from it all. Spending time outside in the natural world is one of the best prescriptions for our overall health and happiness. Everyone should get their daily dose of it!" He stopped to laugh at his own antics.

"It seems these days our lives are so scheduled that we rarely have a moment to collect our thoughts. Between the demands of work, family, and social activities, who can find the time for personal contemplation and connecting with our true spirit? And, even when free moments do arise, we often fill the time with television or other activities that take us away from the natural world, " Bob said. His playful mood gave way to a more serious tone.

"Yeah, I'm certainly guilty of watching too much TV," I admitted.

"There is nothing wrong with watching television, but too much can rob us of living life while watching someone else pretend on TV. We get a lot more from being outside and enjoying the beauty that surrounds us. The English poet, Phillip James Bailey said, 'Art is man's nature; nature is God's art.' I think the most beautiful landscape is the rolling hills of Scotland, and I have longed all my life to visit there. In fact, before I forget, I wanted to lend you one of my favorite books; it just happens to be about Scotland," he said, reaching in the side compartment of his golf bag. He handed me a worn book titled *The Linklands*.

"I know you'll really appreciate this story, and I felt compelled to share it with you. You know I'm always listening to that small, still voice we talked about so many weeks ago at our very first lesson. That seems like it was so long ago. Well, I guess when you start getting older time seems to pass too quickly." Bob choked up; he was visibly upset about something. He quickly recovered and smiled broadly at me as if everything was good again.

"This reminds me of a story about *The Great Li River*." Bob said in his familiar story voice:

> In ancient China lived an artist whose paintings were almost life-like. The artist's fame had made him proud and conceited. One day the emperor wanted to get his portrait done. He called all great artists to come and present their finest work, so that he could choose the best.
>
> The artist was sure he would be chosen, but when he presented his masterpiece to the emperor's chief minister, the old man laughed. The wise old man told him to travel to the Li River, perhaps he could learn a little from the greatest artist in the world. Reduced to tears with anger and curiosity, the artist packed his bags and left to find out this mysterious master.
>
> When he asked the villagers on the banks of the river for the whereabouts of the legendary artist, they smiled and pointed down the river. The next morning he hired a boat and set out to find the illustrious painter. As the small

boat moved gently along the river, he was left speechless by myriad mountains being silently reflected in the water. He passed milky white waterfalls and mountains in many shades of blue. And when he saw the mists rising from the river and merging with the soft clouds surrounding the peaks, he was reduced to tears. The artist was finally humbled by the greatest artist on earth, Mother Nature.

He paused and continued, "Just like the natural world, Gena, you have that same kind of natural reservoir inside every cell of your being. By gradually cultivating your relationship with nature you will find a feeling of peaceful serenity permeating your soul. The singing birds, the rustling leaves, even a bubbling brook can evoke a quiet tranquility within our spirit that links us with the divine. By connecting with nature we can direct our lives inward and connect with what's most important to us by accessing a larger part of ourselves in relationship to the universe as a whole.

"When you spend time outdoors, especially being active, you can lift your mood, think more positively, feel calmer, and experience greater harmony with the world around you." Out of breath after his long discourse, Bob sat on the bench near the greens.

"I totally agree with everything you've said, Bob. One of the greatest experiences Dad ever gave me was teaching me to appreciate nature at an early age. Every year he would take my six older brothers and me up into the mountains. We backpacked into the high sierras for a couple weeks at time. Sometimes we'd pack in with horses, while other times we would just hike by foot with our packs on our back." I smiled, fondly remembering those precious times.

"During the day we crossed streams, riverbeds, meadows, valleys and hiked to the nearby lakes. We fished for our dinner, and then at night we'd set up camp and prepare for passing storms. The weather was always unpredictable in the mountains. We'd look up at the stars in the sky and sit around the campfire. My dad said he took us on these trips so that we could attune ourselves to nature and everything that is *within* us," I recalled.

"It sounds like he gave you a wonderful foundation to build upon." Bob always reminded me how blessed I was by my parents.

"I didn't always appreciate that growing up. During these excursions, I became more aware of the mystery of the circle of life and my part in it. In the mornings, Dad pointed out the rising sun and explained how the sun gives life to all things. He'd explain that the sun doesn't compare; it doesn't have favorites. It just gives life through unconditional Love. I see now that Dad took us to the mountains so that we could experience God—The Living Spirit—for ourselves. He worked long, hard hours at his home-based business when I was growing up, but he always created time to take my brothers and me on these treasured trips. He definitely taught me how to connect with the natural world and with God by being in the wonder and the mystery of it all," I said, remembering.

"He taught me to appreciate and enjoy the beauty and the great miracle of life that is also a part of me. Dad was a great teacher in this area of my life. I didn't realize it until our conversation today how much of a gift this truly was and is to me," I said.

"This experience was and is a 'Grand Blessing' that your dad passed on to you, Gena," he said.

"Your father was providing you with all the experiences you needed to propel you to higher ground early in life so that you would become an instrument of Love and serve the divine nature that is within you. Not many children get the privilege to experience what you were able to firsthand. Today the lives of children are much different than they used to be back in the day."

As he pondered which insights to share, a sadness crept over his face.

"Gena, I'm sure you know that throughout most of history, children were free to explore the nearest wild place, whether it was a big tree or brushy area in the yard, or a pond or the woods. Not that long ago, most children spent their days surrounded by fields, farms, and nature, soaking up the sunshine and experiences of living creatures and growing things. Children had the freedom to play, explore, and interact with the natural world with little or no restriction or adult supervision."

As I listened to Bob, I remembered spending time on my Aunt Donna's property, catching frogs, fishing, climbing trees, and making up games with rocks and sticks. At the end of the day, we'd be mud-splattered, hungry, exhausted, and as happy as a child could be. "It is a great loss for kids today not ever to experience that kind of carefree roaming in nature." I took on Bob's regretful tone when I said this.

Bob went on, "Many working families can't supervise their children after school, so you have kids who stay indoors and watch TV, play video games, or attend supervised after-school programs and over-structured activities like sports or dance. It seems to me that children's lives have become so structured and so scheduled by adults that they have no time left to just be kids," he said, shaking his head. "I sure didn't mean to get on my soapbox today, but I knew you'd understand, and maybe you'll be able to help others see the great mistake being made for the next generation. I sense you will be someone who others will turn to for wisdom, someone who will touch and change lives."

I suddenly felt my calling, my mission in life rising within. Bob made me feel as if I could actually make a difference and lead people to a more purposeful lifestyle. I felt empowered and frightened at the same time.

"Your father has gifted you and your brothers with a priceless treasure that will be a part of your spirit and your memories forever. Use these gifts for yourself and bless others with them," he said in a caring tone.

I left the golf course that day with a deeper understanding of who I was and what I would be doing with my life.

Dearest One,

Bob showed me how I could be more peaceful and joyful in the midst of a full and demanding schedule. Focused on my new career and concerned about moving upward in my company, while attending school, I poured all my energy into creating a solid foundation for myself. I gave 100% to work and school in those days, leaving no time for *me*.

I attended night school because I was an avid learner. I enrolled in writing classes, psychology classes, philosophy classes, art classes, and others. In a sense, I created my own busy-ness. I did not fully understand that slowing down, finding time to relax, and maintaining a healthy *balance* was in my best interest. I pushed forward fast and hard without ever pausing to rest.

I learned my lesson the hard way when I burned out from exhaustion and fatigue, all because of my *own* doing. Early in my career, I placed a lot of undue pressure on myself, causing the chaotic feeling of anxiety and panic that I experienced. I was responsible for creating this crazy, demanding schedule and causing my own stress.

Bob offered profound wisdom when he suggested I take the time for personal contemplation and reflection. If I didn't, I would eventually lose touch with my spirit and innermost purpose as a result.

He reminded me that getting in touch with nature improves our emotional and mental well-being as well as our physical health. Connecting with nature is healing to the mind, body, and spirit. It slows us down, takes us out of our normal routines, and reminds us that we live on a remarkable, beautiful planet. Nature surrounds us with countless signs of God's presence. Being outside in nature inspires feelings of awe and wonder and acquaints us with our higher self by placing us in direct connection with our true spirit. Nature is a source of solace, healing, insight, and regeneration. Here we can be inspired, recharge our batteries, and live in direct relationship with God and Mother Earth.

Here's a snapshot of my typical day of work and school, while I took golf lessons with Bob:

5:00AM: Rise and shine, shower and dress. Do homework, organize my books and class notes. Sometimes grab a quick breakfast at a fast-food restaurant on my way to work.

7AM - 5PM: Work, work, work with barely enough time to eat, and never eating well when I did.

6:00PM – 8PM: Night School Classes

8PM: Grab a quick fast food dinner on my way home from school.

9PM-10PM: Last-minute reading/studying before bed.

Dear God,
Nature is so perfect.
Nature doesn't suffer or stress.
It just accepts everything.
Everything is drawn together through it.

Chapter 14
Good Nutrition

Dear God,
May I learn to care for my body
in a way that's loving, nourishing,
and kind.

We started our lesson on the bench at the first hole. I wanted Bob's advice on something I had been thinking about on the drive over. "Bob, over the years I have accumulated a lot of bad eating habits. When I'm anxious or stressed, I have a tendency not to eat very much or anything at all for that matter. When I lived at home, I had so much anxiety and worry that I felt out of control most of the time. How do I create healthier lifestyle habits that support the well-being of my body?" I asked intently.

Bob was happy to offer his advice on the topic. "Sometimes we can unintentionally develop unhealthy eating habits in order to compensate for the lack of control we feel in other areas of our lives. Food just isn't appealing especially when we are anxious, worried, or feeling hopeless about a particular situation.

"The downfall to this is that not eating enough can make you more irritable and sensitive, which can intensify your moods and feelings of anxiety, stress, or worry," he pointed out. "When you play a sport like golf, or any sport for that matter, you need to ensure that you have the proper equipment to play your very best. It's the same way with your nutritional needs. You have to keep yourself fueled up with the proper kinds of food in order to have enough energy to play your very best."

"I'm totally with you on this and that is why I ate two meals today," I teased, teeing off.

"What did you have to eat today?" Bob asked a little hesitantly.

"I had a glazed donut and a cup of milk for breakfast, and for lunch I hit the drive-thru window at Burger King and had a quick burger with fries and a diet coke," I claimed.

"I'm sure you realize that just eating to get something in your stomach and healthy eating are not the same things. Healthy eating means choosing a variety of balanced foods that give you the nutrients you need to maintain your health, vitality, and energy levels. Balanced nutrition is important for everyone, not just us golfers," Bob replied.

"Oh, I'm a proper golfer now?" I laughed.

"You're playing golf, aren't you?" He chuckled before continuing. "Eating healthy, balanced meals provides nutrients to your body. These nutrients give you energy and keep your heart beating, your brain active, and your muscles working effectively all day long."

"What do you mean by eating a variety of balanced meals?" admitting my ignorance on this subject matter.

Bob took his professorial stance and said, "Food is broken down into three categories: carbohydrates, proteins, and fats. A balanced meal requires all of these food groups to ensure that proper nutrients are being supplied to our body."

"I don't even know what those words mean. Carbohydrates, proteins, and fats? Well, I know what fat means when it goes directly to my hips," I said, laughing at my own joke.

Bob couldn't help but laugh with me and said, "That's not exactly the kind of fat I'm talking about, Gena, so I'll give you a quick breakdown of the food groups and why they are important."

Bob continued, "Carbohydrates include beans, whole grains, fruits and vegetables. These foods provide the 'energy' our body and brain need to function properly throughout the day.

"These are all live, natural foods that are created through the interaction of the sun, air, soil, and water. Eating whole, live, nutrient-rich carbohydrate foods can assist our body's ability to rid itself of toxins and enhance its energetic field."

He went on and said, "Protein consists of beef, fish, chicken, and dairy products such as milk, yogurt, eggs and even vegetables that contain some protein. Protein provides our body with amino acids, which build and repair our body on a daily basis. This includes our hair, skin, nails and muscle tissue."

"Cool! I didn't know that," I said, surprised I was remotely interested in talking about food.

"It *is* cool, and that is why it's so important to include some form of protein in your meal planning every day," he insisted.

He went on to say, "Some healthy fat is also needed in our body to keep blood sugar balanced while also keeping us feeling full for longer periods of time. Healthy fats include things like nuts, oils, and fish. Some people are sensitive to certain foods like dairy or wheat, but a balanced diet can still be supported when you're properly educated."

> ***"Healthy eating is not about depriving yourself of the foods you love; it's about practicing balance and moderation.***

"An eating program that is too restrictive on calories or food choices is not sustainable and sets us up for all kind of problems down the road. Finding a healthy balance for your own individual body requirements may take some experimenting, but it's well worth the effort for your overall well-being. Does any of this make sense to you?" Bob looked at me to ensure I understood.

"Yes, it sure does, and I can see now that I don't eat balanced meals. At work for example, I'll either skip lunch altogether or eat fast food at my desk in a mad hurry," I admitted.

"First off, it's not a good idea to skip meals because in doing this, you are slowing down your metabolism. Your metabolism controls the energy required for your heart to beat, along with other metabolic functions like maintaining your internal temperature, repairing your cells, pumping your blood and powering your muscles. When you have a slow metabolism, you will not have the energy to work effectively throughout your day. This is because your body is using up whatever energy it has left to keep your metabolic functions operating at normal levels.

"When you eat healthy balanced meals throughout the course of your day, this helps to increase your energy levels and to keep your blood sugar levels regulated," he explained.

"That explains why I'm so low on energy most of the time. I just thought I was a low energy person," I said, realizing I needed to start making some changes soon.

"French lawyer and politician Jean Anthelme Brillat-Savarin said; 'Tell me what you eat, and I will tell you what you are.'"

"Touché," I said laughing.

Bob approached the tee box. "You might think that eating at your desk will help to decrease the long lists of tasks that you need to complete, but eating lunch at your desk is just not good for your health in the same way that skipping meals is not good for you. Leaving your desk for lunch allows your mind to unwind and recharge so you can take on the second half of the day," he reminded me.

"Gulping down nutritionally deprived food at your desk causes your digestive system to become inflamed, acidic, and tense, so time away from your desk could be taken to enjoy a healthy, balanced meal. And the end result will be a much more pleasant one. The key to healthy eating is to become very *conscious* of your food intake and how your body feels in response to those foods. If you eat at your desk while working, you are building a habit of eating without awareness, which is also called unconscious eating," he explained.

"I have never thought about any of this before. I just eat and never give it a second thought," I replied.

"Yes, eating to tantalize your taste buds and not paying attention to how the food will affect your physical system, eating when you aren't hungry, eating more than you intended, eating in a hurry or on the go, eating under an emotional state of stress or anxiety, eating too quickly, eating often in front of the TV or at your desk are all symptoms of unconscious eating. Many people eat in front of the television or at their desk and check out mentally. It's like your body is there, but your consciousness is riveted to whatever is on TV or displayed on your computer screen," he pointed out.

"Because of this, you eat and eat and are not even aware of how much you have eaten. Worse yet, you don't even think about what types of food you are putting into your body. Unconscious eating, or eating without awareness, can have some negative health consequences in the long run," Bob made clear to me.

"What kind of negative health consequences?" I really wanted to know.

"If you are not aware of what you are eating—say you eat too much sugar—your energetic vitality will lower which over time causes digestive imbalances in your body. This causes faster use of pancreatic-digestive enzymes and can cause gas, bloating, belching, constipation, diarrhea and even heartburn as well as muscle pain, skin disorders, and insomnia," he justified.

"That doesn't sound pleasant at all!" I said.

"It's not, but it can be easily remedied with a little bit of awareness and by taking positive action to prevent it. The French author La Rochefoucauld said it best: 'To eat is a necessity, but to eat intelligently is an art.'"

Dearest One,

I must admit it took me many years to break free from my unhealthy eating habits. While I did not struggle with being overweight like so many others, my body was so undernourished from eating nutrient deficient foods for so many years that I suffered the negative side effects of extreme stress, fatigue, mental fogginess, lethargy, headaches, and mood swings.

Bob taught me to see the body as a miracle from God that we should love and nourish. We need to optimize our health by giving our bodies positive and loving nourishment with the foods we eat, the thoughts we think, and the daily habits we form.

Healthy eating is not about strict nutritional philosophies or about depriving ourselves of the foods we love; rather, it's about feeling great, having more energy, and keeping our mental and physical well-being as healthy as possible for life!

I learned and embodied this lesson at a higher level when I left my corporate job in 2006 to pursue a career in health and wellness.

There was no particular opportunity that allowed me to leave the corporate world for the field of health and wellness other than the opportunity of *change.*

I desperately wanted to leave my company four years prior to my mom's passing in 2005, but I didn't have the courage to do so. At that time, I didn't know what direction to take professionally, so I stayed with my company because I didn't have a *clear* calling.

My mom's battle with pancreatic cancer was the catalyst that made me ultimately decide to move into the field of health and wellness after she transitioned.

My mom's death was always my *worst fear* from the moment she attempted suicide when I was nine years old. Prior to her passing, I was terrified of loss in general, and I was also terrified of *change.* I was afraid to leave my company and learn something new because I had so much invested in my career of 18 years. I identified myself through my career, and I also felt secure in the money and the health benefits it provided.

In 2001, four years prior to my mom's passing, my brother Bobbie took his life. He suffered from on-going depression, and his heartbreaking death affected me profoundly. This affected my *entire* family deeply, and in some cases, I may never know how deeply. My mom and dad were completely heartbroken from the loss of their son.

Both these losses took a devastating toll on me physically, spiritually, and mentally. I felt myself slowly slipping into a state of depression after the passing of both my brother and my mom. My dad's health was spiraling downhill at that time due to his battle with Parkinson's disease. Because of this, I knew I had to make a significant change in order to pull myself up and out of my own state of depression before the negative energy completely took over my spirit. It was during this time that I remembered all of Bob's lessons and everything he taught me. His lessons flooded back, and I could hear his voice encouraging me to press forward in the spirit of Love.

At that time in my career, I saved enough money to pursue a new career in health and wellness. I enrolled in a college where I studied anatomy, physiology, pathology, nutrition, sports medicine, lifestyle coaching and fitness training. It was also during that time in my life when I met my husband *Bob Livings*, an amazing man and a true blessing in my life.

Today, I get to do what I love for a living. I spend my time sharing and expressing myself through writing, while inspiring others to achieve a lifestyle that promotes health and wellness as a better way of life!

In 2009, I wrote "Inspired Wellness – The Livings Key Principles for Creating Wholeness, Peace and Health from the Inside Out." This free online guide is an outline for *Saturdays With Bob: Life Changing Golf Lessons for Mind, Body and Spirit*. The principles presented in this short work are simply the insights Bob bestowed upon me in generalized terms without telling the story of Bob and our time together. Please feel free to visit me at www.GenaLivings.com to receive your free copy.

In 2013, I wrote *Eat Healthy for Balance and Wholeness – A Conscious Food Guide for Building Awareness and Honoring Your Body Temple.*

Dear God,
I see my body as a miracle from you that I
Love and want to nourish.
May my life be a living expression of
love, health, happiness, vitality
and well-being.

CHAPTER 15

Healthy Exercise—the Final Lesson

On the drive over, I looked at our golf lessons as a bit of a workout; however, I realized that I wasn't getting enough exercise since I spent most of my time sedentary, trapped behind my desk.

Bob greeted me with his usual warm smile, but he said, "Gena, I'm feeling a little tuckered out today. Let's sit a spell and visit before we get started. I actually wanted to talk to you today about one of my favorite subjects."

I was a little concerned for Bob since he always seemed so full of vitality. In fact, I usually had a hard time keeping up with him. "Is everything alright, Bob?" I asked, genuinely concerned.

"I'm just fine but getting a little slower these days. Nothing at all to fuss about. And actually it leads me right into what I wanted to talk about," he said. "Last week, we discussed the importance of fueling your body with healthy nutrition. Maintaining a healthy lifestyle also includes getting out and moving your body on a daily basis. I think the game of golf has served this old body of mine well, and I'm grateful to have been given this precious time."

We sat in silence for a while and a familiar feeling of stillness and peace washed over me before Bob continued. "Golfing," he said, "is sometimes thought of as a passive sport that does not require any real degree of exercise, but in reality, golf incorporates cardiovascular exercise, strength training, and even balance and coordination skills. With all these benefits, it's hard to say no to a game of golf. The sport of golf also requires a lot of walking. With 18 holes, the average golf course is between five and eight miles. If you keep a brisk pace while walking from hole to hole, you can definitely get in a good cardio workout."

He added, "Carrying your own clubs counts as a weight-bearing exercise, and when used in conjunction with walking you will cause your heart to beat faster. Taking care of your physical body is a powerful step toward mental, emotional, and spiritual well-being and is all part of a healthy lifestyle. This is because your mind, body, and spirit are linked. For example, exercise not only strengthens your heart and lungs but also releases endorphins, which are powerful chemicals that will energize you and lift your spirits and your mood. Part of the success of exercise involves rejecting the mainstream crowd and getting comfortable just doing what's healthy, fun, and enjoyable for you, regardless of the latest fitness craze."

"I totally agree!" I interrupted Bob. "I like all kinds of exercise and many different sports. I'd get bored if I only did one thing over and over again. I'm not too fond of running, but I love playing golf, riding my bike, swimming, roller-skating, shooting hoops, and hiking."

"Exactly my point! Grinding through a rigid, one-dimensional fitness program will do little for you," Bob agreed. "Shake it up a little. Remember, our physical activity is meant to add passion and pleasure to our lives, not take away from it. This must always, always be the goal of a healthy exercise program. A common misconception about exercise is that it must be regimented, almost devoid of enjoyment. This is an absolutely untrue myth! Anything at all that gets your heart humming is considered aerobic exercise," he clarified. "If and when you grow tired of your exercise, seize the moment, act on your childlike impulses, and pick another sport. The idea is to keep an exciting amount of variety in your fitness plan and not be afraid to try out new things. If you hate aerobic dance, don't join an aerobics class."

"That seems pretty logical, but I have friends that hate their aerobics classes, yet they force themselves through them as if they don't have a choice," I shared.

Bob went on, "If you hate going to the gym for structured fitness classes, don't go there. There are so many options; the choices are literally endless."

"I much prefer being outside in the fresh air than being stuck in a smelly gym," I said.

Bob nodded in agreement and said, "Exactly, and if you hate working out on home exercise machines, don't buy one. Most of them do little for our long-term fitness anyway and end up under the bed or drying wet clothes. Physiologically, there is very little difference between the benefits you would derive from any of the popular home exercise machines and those from a good, steady helping of push-up, sit-ups along with a brisk walk. Becoming a more healthy and happy person is the path toward a lifestyle of health and well-being.

Gena, I know this will probably surprise you, but I have a story for you," he said with a grin.

> There is a group of monks called the Tendai "marathon monks," also known as Kaihigyo.
>
> They are spiritual athletes from the Tendai Sect of Buddhism, based at Mount Hiei, which overlooks the ancient capital city of Kyoto.
>
> These monks are best known for their great spiritual effort and perseverance in ascetic practices.
>
> The Tendai run one full marathon (26.2 miles) every day for one hundred days as their path to spiritual enlightenment.
>
> You have to admit that this is an awe-inspiring physical feat even to professional runners.
>
> But the Tendai don't just cover a lot of miles, they see running as much more, as each step is another opportunity to learn more about themselves, to go deeper 'inside.'

> *Running used as a form of exercise is their way to complete self-awareness.*

Bob paused and added, "In America, most of us don't view exercise in this way. We talk about burning calories and chatter about looking thin and managing our weight. We step on the treadmill, hit the little green button, turn off our minds, and begin counting. That is one reason our exercise doesn't inspire us. When we focus on the superficial benefits of exercise (weight loss, quicker running times, etc.), there is an immediate disconnect between body and mind. That makes sticking to an exercise program, for the most of us, far more difficult," Bob explained.

"For the Tendai monks, the calories burned aren't the focus; the calories burned are a natural result of the passion-driven activity. The passion and performance approach shift our perspective to one that is much more motivating. So we need to see exercise for what it can be: a unique opportunity for personal growth, a celebration of life, a walk into the world, and part of the total journey! There is one certainty in life: We live in this body until this body eventually wears out and dies. We have a choice to live in a body that helps us reach our full potential, or in one that limits us," Bob said, enlightening me.

"I don't think that I could ever become as disciplined as the the Tendai *marathon monks* to run 26.2 miles every day for one hundred days, but their story sure is inspiring," I admitted.

Bob laughed hard. "Not too many people could be like the Tendai, but a little bit of healthy exercise surely does go a long way. Seeing exercise as a joyful experience, a unique opportunity for personal growth, and a celebration of life is the key to achieving a healthy lifestyle."

Dearest One,

In our final lesson together, Bob taught me to see exercise as joyful movement, not necessarily something that you have to perform for long painful hours at a gym. Exercise is more about paying attention to the rhythms and sensations you experience in your body as you move. While exercise is often promoted as a way to lose weight and achieve an idealized body shape, it also often helps us feel good in our bodies, which in turn can help us accept and even celebrate how we look and feel.

I love this quote by Carol Welch:

> *"Movement is a medicine for creating change in a person's physical, emotional, and mental states."*

CHAPTER 16
Conclusion

Our final lesson where Bob talked about healthy exercise was the last time I ever saw Bob. He exited my life as unexpectedly as he entered it. It was two weeks after our final lesson when I realized I was still holding onto the book that he loaned me. I opened up the front jacket and inside was a handwritten note from one of his former students: *'From a friend and an appreciative student ~ Rich'*

It was Saturday, so I decided to take a drive to Napa to return the book. I admit that I already missed our time together. When I arrived at the range, there was no sign of Bob anywhere, so I asked one of the workers if I could leave the book for Bob to pick up on his next visit to the course.

The worker said, "Bob is no longer here. He moved on."

It took me a moment to process what he said. Bob never mentioned anything to me about moving on. "What do you mean he moved on?" I asked.

"Bob just told me that he was moving on and that's all I know," the worker said and walked away.

That's so strange, I thought to myself, and I wondered if my dad knew anything about Bob's sudden disappearance from the golf course. I drove to the Veteran's Home to see Dad, but when I told him the news, he was just as surprised as I was. Dad and I had lunch together that afternoon, and we talked about many of the ideas Bob shared with me over the past twelve months.

"Dad, I learned so much from Bob. And I'm so grateful you decided to introduce us. It seems like I was destined to spend this special time with him. Not only did he teach me his amazing golf swing, but he also shared with me some powerful insights to help me live an inspired life.

During our hours of discussions, he helped me to discover my mission in life. I feel so blessed for our time together and grateful to you for arranging it," I said excitedly.

"I'd love to hear all the details, tell me everything you remember, Honey. I want to know if you were paying attention," he said with a mischievous grin. "Seriously, I'd love to hear all about it. I have all the time in the world!" Dad leaned back into the recliner and said very softly, "Swing away…"

"Did you just say, 'Swing away'?" I was taken by surprise.

"Yeah, why?" he asked gently.

"That's what Bob would say when I was about to say something." I suddenly felt a sense of loss when I realized all that Bob had come to mean to me, and I didn't know at that moment if our paths would cross again. We sat in silence for a little while as Dad waited for me to regain my composure. At that moment I felt Bob's presence and remembered how he taught me to look within for answers. I knew a little bit of Bob would be with me wherever I went.

I thought about the lesson Bob taught me on living in the present moment and realized Dad and I had a lot of catching up to do. I shared with him some of the highlights of Bob's teachings and how each seemed to come at exactly the moment I needed to hear them to endure some personal struggle or to help me make a big decision. It was uncanny how each session felt as if he knew things he couldn't possibly know. "Does that make sense, Dad?" I asked, wondering if I sounded a bit crazy.

We laughed together and had one of the best visits ever. Dad and I decided to make Saturdays our day to spend some quality time together. This was just another fruit of my time with Bob in learning to appreciate and savor precious moments.

The cherished time that I spent with Bob radically changed my outlook and gave me a whole new approach to life. I don't know where I would be today *internally* if I didn't have that one-year experience, a miracle and a blessing beyond imagining.

I have an enormous amount of gratitude still today for this opportunity and all of Bob's wisdom it *changed* me. It changed my life and the way I see the world today. Hopefully, these lessons will continue to reach and bless many…Bob's wisdom lives on in each of us.

Some people come into our lives in order to make a lasting impression and then quietly fade away.

Some people come into our lives to penetrate our souls, wake us up, and move our hearts toward love.

Some people come into our lives to guide us to new understandings with the passing whisper of their wisdom.

Some people come into our lives in order to make the days more beautiful, to enrich our spirits, and to leave a message on our Hearts.

We don't know what we have in these people until we lose them, and we don't know what we've been missing until they arrive.

Each person who comes into our life bestows a gift, a blessing, and a purpose. We are all Instruments of God's Love!

This is not the End....this is a New Beginning!

Dearest One:

After our final lesson together it never occurred to me that this would be the last time that I would ever see Bob again so I never said a final goodbye. Oddly enough, I have very little memory of the conversation that ended our time together. All I know is that I was extremely grateful to him for all his teachings, so much so, that I couldn't fully express myself in words. One thing is certain: I experienced a profound miracle and healing in my life. I believe to this day that my Saturday's with Bob and his life changing golf lessons were a blessing, a gift and an answer to prayer.

Dear God,
Thank you
for answering
my prayers.

Gratitudes

*Deep gratitude to my Creator, God.
My source of life and giver of love.*

God has blessed me with teachers and angels who have all inspired me to live my best life! I especially feel deep gratitude for my beloved parents. Although they have transitioned from this physical world, they continue to guide my way and support my passage. I give thanks to my six older brothers for being my fellow journeyers and guardians and to my husband, Bob, for loving, supporting, and believing in me always. Big thanks to my clients and friends who have all blessed my life with their special wisdom, beauty, and grace. And of course, there's Bob, who taught me to love life, to trust my inner-guidance, and to pursue my Highest Calling.

About the Author

Gena Livings is a spiritual practitioner of healthy living and the founder of GenaLivings.com. She is also the author *of Eat Healthy for Balance and Wholeness – A Conscious Food Guide for Building Awareness and Honoring Your Body Temple* and the complementary on-line guidebook, "The Livings Key Principles – For Creating Wholeness, Peace and Health from the Inside Out!"

Gena radically redesigned her life after spending eighteen years in a high-stress corporate environment that left her body and spirit utterly depleted. She studied anatomy, physiology, pathology, sports medicine, nutrition, lifestyle modification coaching, and fitness training before obtaining her certification as a personal trainer and health and wellness professional. She now supports private clients and a growing on-line community with heart-centered, easy and practical ways to balance mind, body, and spirit.

Gena Livings is available for Speaking Engagements, Radio Interviews and Television Appearances by visiting http://www.genalivings.com
or call (530) 906-1990 for customized programs

Other Books Written By Gena:

- A FREE online hand-guide entitled "Inspired Wellness – The Livings Key Principles for Creating Wholeness, Peace and Health From the Inside Out"

- Eat Healthy for Balance and Wholeness – A Conscious Food Guide for Building Awareness and Honoring Your Body Temple

Today Gena does what she loves by expressing herself through writing and inspiring others to achieve a lifestyle that promotes health and well-being as a better way of life. As a lifestyle modification coach and a spiritual practitioner of healthy living, she helps people cultivate their awareness so that they can make conscious lifestyle choices based on healthy lifestyle practices and a healthy mind-set.

Be sure to connect with Gena on Facebook at
https://www.facebook.com/GenasHealthyLiving

www.ingramcontent.com/pod-product-compliance
Lightning Source LLC
Chambersburg PA
CBHW061644040426
42446CB00010B/1579